HEART
SONG

By Scott Gray
Published by Ballantine Books:

HEART SONG: The Story of Jewel

Books published by The Ballantine Publishing Group
are available at quantity discounts on bulk purchases
for premium, educational, fund-raising, and special
sales use. For details, please call 1-800-733-3000.

HEART SONG

The Story of Jewel

Scott Gray

BALLANTINE BOOKS • NEW YORK

A Ballantine Book
Published by The Ballantine Publishing Group
Copyright © 1998 by Scott Gray
Cover photo © Norman Ng/Outline Press

http://www.randomhouse.com

Library of Congress Catalog Card Number: 98-96159

ISBN 0-345-42678-9

Manufactured in the United States of America

First Ballantine Books Edition: June 1998

10 9 8 7 6 5 4 3 2 1

Contents

Contents

Contents

Acknowledgments

My friend says, "If you succeeded, you had help; if you failed, you did it on your own." It takes a team of dedicated professionals to make a book, and I've been lucky enough to have the very best helping me on this one.

Cathy Repetti is an extraordinary editor whom I'm proud to also call my friend. Mark Rifkin is a shepherd of lost books and a great person to boot. In fact, all the folks at Ballantine are worthy of fanfare: George Davidson, Betsy Elias, Steve Palmer, and Caron Harris.

Christopher Colley lent vast insight into the essence of Alaska, while Heather Poort provided extensive research into just about everything else.

Thank you, Mom and Dad!

Preface

"I'm always portrayed in the media as a naive
twenty-two-year-old trying to
impress adults. What can I say?"
—Jewel Kilcher in *LAUNCHonline*

"I'm still learning. I have no pretense
of having arrived."
—Jewel in *The Boston Globe*

"But I have a dream I want to live out
that isn't relevant to age."
—Jewel in *NewTimes*

Playwright and critic George Bernard Shaw once wrote, "The reasonable man adapts himself to the world; the unreasonable one persists in trying to adapt the world to himself. Therefore, all progress depends on the unreasonable man."

Or woman. For me, the unspoken lesson of Jewel's life is that you should pursue your passions, no matter what the obstacles, no matter what the world defines as unreasonable. In the end, it all comes down to following your heart, even if well-intentioned people tell you you're a fool. Life is never going to be easy; in fact, it'll be tougher than you can realize until it's too late to turn back. So you might as well take relish in the struggle. As Jewel once said in an interview with talk show host Jon Stewart, "I'm in love with the fight . . . the good fight."

A comparatively young person who happens to have had more life experience than most folks twice her age, Jewel seems uniquely qualified to speak to the hearts of people of all ages; not from on high but as an artist with a wise and unusual perspective.

When asked by Charlie Rose what advice she would give to her younger fans, Jewel responded by pointing out that "there really aren't mistakes." She went on to advise, "Be very adventurous and brave in your life. Love bravely, live bravely, be courageous; there's really nothing to lose. There's no wrong you can't make right again, so be kinder to yourself . . . have fun, take chances. There's no bounds." That's worthwhile advice for anyone, young or old.

Of course, Jewel never intended to live a lesson, unspoken or otherwise. As she puts it: "All I do is live my life, and people take from it what they get. . . ." Thankfully, she does it in a way that can inspire others to walk a path similar to the one she has taken.

And isn't that the essence of being an artist: to live with blitzkrieg intensity and attempt to send out word of the experience to those who might decide to join you. Sort of an advance scout of the spiritual. As she often says, "We live our lives in front of each other . . . all you can do is be honest."

I regret that Jewel didn't have a hand in the writing of *Heart Song*—it is by definition an unauthorized biography—yet the book would clearly not exist but for her courage and artistry. In that regard she has my heartfelt gratitude. *Heart Song* is dedicated to Everyday Angels everywhere, among whom I am happy to be included.

PROLOGUE

❦

Setting: The Stage

A young woman stands alone in a spotlight, surrounded by lovely red roses and flickering faux candles—the only accoutrements on an otherwise bare stage. She is a vision of grace, a word that she has defined as "the refinement of a soul over time." Her warm, spontaneous smile reaches out through the darkness of a packed concert hall.

Each member of the audience feels the electricity of her presence. Her sincerity and verve shine and sparkle in the hearts of those who've come to celebrate her music. She has earned their adoration with her songs and stories, and now they wait patiently, hushed in anticipation.

Holding a bright blue acoustic guitar, she takes a long drink of water, then gathers her breath and tells the capacity crowd, "I love my life, and I want to thank you all for caring about me." The fans cheer wildly as she begins to play a song, "Deep Water," that she has dedicated to them. With a voice that swings effortlessly from joyful heights to soulful valleys, she sings of how it feels to be immersed in an ocean of troubles, concluding that life is ultimately "nothing without love."

This remarkable young woman, whose poetic songwriting and angelic voice have touched listeners all over the world, is, of course, Jewel Kilcher, known to millions simply as Jewel. But the question remains: just who is Jewel? Is it possible that this person who has spoken to the hearts of so many strangers once had the following experience?

> "[A Native American family] took me
> out to a meadow and said, 'Your life in
> the future will call for you to speak honestly to
> people. You don't know how
> to speak from your heart, and you need
> to learn how.' I was crying because
> I couldn't say anything sincere."

Ultimately it might be said that Jewel's life so far has been a continuous journey during which she learned how to speak—and sing—from the heart. It's been a winding, difficult path, but she has maintained her innocence, found a sense of purpose, and fulfilled her destiny. Anyone who has ever dreamed of blazing his or her own trail to freedom can take inspiration from the amazing story of Jewel.

... a few sweep of three notes on the
... sky, she had done it. With the splitting
... whole voice tears the emotion...

CHAPTER ONE

A National Treasure

"I may look very dramatic and passionate,
and up and down, but damn, I know
myself and I'm grappling with everything that
comes up, and I'll say it. . . . That's my trip."
—Jewel in *Soda*

Legendary rock writer Lester Bangs suggested that the crucial question for the future was whether humans would still have emotions. It's anyone's guess what Lester would say about the state of modern music as we approach the new millennium, but it's a safe bet that he'd have appreciated Jewel's efforts to throw open the floodgates of emotion.

And he wouldn't be alone. With sales of her debut CD, *Pieces of You,* surpassing eight million and counting, Jewel is arguably the most popular woman in popular music. Incredibly, *Pieces of You* sold over 4.3 million copies in 1997 alone—more than two years after its initial date of release!

Jewel's photogenic face has been on the front covers of dozens of magazines, from *Time* to *Rolling Stone*. She has made countless appearances on television talk shows, from Leno to Letterman. She was a main-stage performer during two stretches of 1997–98 critically acclaimed Lilith Fair summer megatour. And she completed sold-out solo stints in Europe and Asia that winter. Jewel even has a starring role in an upcoming motion picture. A collection of her poetry is scheduled for release in late 1998.

Jewel's appeal crosses all boundaries, a rare feat in today's niche-driven markets. The qualities that make her songs beautiful—poignant lyrics, memorable instrumentation, and pop music's most mesmerizing voice—touch every type of person, regardless of sex, age, religion, or race.

Attending one of her live performances, it isn't uncommon to see entire families together, singing along with Jewel and a roomful of strangers, bonded by musical and spiritual harmony. Fans from across Europe, Australia, Asia, and America have filled clubs and concert halls to hear Jewel sing and play.

She has also been hailed by critics for her spectacular voice and creative songwriting. Her work has been nominated for numerous honors, including a trio of Grammy Awards. With the release of her long-awaited second CD, 1998 figures to be Jewel's finest year yet.

But if it all sounds a bit too perfect, don't be fooled. Jewel has earned her phenomenal success not merely with talent but with plenty of sweat and tears as well. Few veterans of the industry have paid more dues than twenty-four-year-old Jewel.

Arguably the most inspiring aspect of Jewel's rise to fame is that she has achieved superstar status without scrapping her beliefs or being anything other than herself. She has remained humble and spontaneous, frequently referring to herself as "a big dork of rock 'n' roll." And to her legions of admirers, she is true blue—the most sincere individual in music.

As always, the journey begins light-years from the glaring flash of fame. As always, the journey begins at home.

CHAPTER TWO

❦

At Land's End

Jewel Kilcher was born on May 23, 1974, to Atz and Lenedra Kilcher, in Payson, Utah. Jewel's brother, Shane, was three years old at the time of Jewel's birth. The Kilchers left Utah while Jewel was still a baby, setting out for a place that made Payson seem like a major population center in comparison—the nation's final frontier: Alaska.

Ceded to the United States by Russia in 1867 for less than two cents per acre, Alaska was ridiculed as "Seward's Folly," after the Secretary of State who arranged the deal. By the end of 1898 the Klondike area of Seward's Folly had yielded some $22 million in gold, and the critics fell curiously silent. A hundred years after the initial purchase, massive reserves of "black gold"—petroleum—were discovered, making the former secretary look like a genius of foresight.

Alaska was the forty-ninth state admitted into

the Union, entering with Hawaii in 1959. The two states have little else in common at first glance, yet there are geographic similarities: the defining presence of the Pacific Ocean, volcanic landscapes and other natural wonders, and isolation from the coterminous United States. Jewel would eventually be exposed to both of these unique places during her formative years.

The largest state in terms of land area, Alaska has the second-smallest population. The harsh weather and forbidding distances make for hearty locals and a large transient population of adventurers and entrepreneurs. Alaska isn't for the faint of heart.

If geography shapes people, it follows that extreme locations can create extraordinary individuals. Alaska is harsh and unforgiving, yet it is also majestic and spectacularly beautiful. It encompasses both isolation and freedom and is above all a place that embraces diversity and rewards self-reliance.

The starkly intense environment seems to spark the creative juices of everyone who has ever called Alaska home. Whether they were natives who carved intricate totem poles or a twentieth-century writer such as Jack London, Alaska has been a never-ending source of artistic inspiration.

It was in this land that Jewel was raised, on an eight-hundred-acre homestead eleven miles east of Homer, Alaska. It doesn't get much more extreme than that, at least not in the United States.

Located on the southwestern Kenai Peninsula, Homer encompasses roughly eleven square miles of land and sixteen square miles of water. Literally where the land ends and the sea begins, it is one of the most striking natural areas in Alaska, and on Earth.

Such an environment couldn't help but spark young Jewel's love and appreciation of nature. She frequently cites the influence that the vast open spaces and unbroken silences had on her spiritual development. "I know what a porcupine sounds like climbing a tree," she explains with reverence.

Unlike in the arctic northern part of the state, the wintertime temperature in Homer usually stays between fourteen and twenty-seven degrees Fahrenheit, and the mercury will climb into the forty-five to sixty-five range during summer. The average annual snow and rainfall is about twenty-eight inches. It may not be the arctic expanse that many outsiders picture when they think of Alaska, but Homer can still become a wee bit dreary for those who crave sunshine, as the currently Rancho Santa Fe–based Jewel obviously does.

She remembers waking up on many an icy cold morning with frosty eyelashes and visible breath, debating with family members about who would be first to make the long trek to the outhouse. A coal stove was the lone source of heat for the house, and there was no plumbing for hot, running water.

Fishing and fish processing are the primary industries in Homer, and there are roughly five hundred licensed commercial fishermen in residence. Jewel learned firsthand about the importance of fish in the lives of the locals and her family. "I'd be canning salmon after school while other kids would be watching *He-Man*," Jewel recalls.

Despite being home to a mere four thousand or so citizens, the town has a regional reputation as an artistic community. Homer boasts dozens of small art galleries, offering everything from landscape oil paintings, wood carvings, and pottery, to jewelry and glass sculptures. The fishermen and artists make for a funky blend of blue-collar work ethic and creativity, qualities that Jewel clearly absorbed.

Jewel's family has her father's father to thank for providing the homestead that they called home. Grandfather Yule, who emigrated to Alaska before it became a state, was a native of Switzerland, a country whose independence dates to 1499.

With some 70 percent of its total land area consisting of the Alps and Jura Mountains, Switzerland has little to offer in terms of natural resources. Its prosperity has been attained through technological innovation, tourism, and the exportation of chocolate and cheese. The Swiss maintained armed neutrality throughout both world wars, and the country boasts a 100 percent literacy rate for its population of roughly eight million.

A typical Swiss immigrant, Yule Kilcher arrived in America an educated, independent person. He has even been credited with helping write the Alaska state charter. He floated down the Yukon River on a homemade raft, making his way to the Kachemak Bay area and laying claim to a tract of land under a homestead act. Jewel's grandparents built a house, cultivated the acreage, and had eight children, one of whom was Jewel's father, Atz.

Coming of age more than two hundred miles from the nearest large city, Atz Kilcher enjoyed a daily communion with nature. He learned how to farm the land, catch fish, and tend horses, and he was exposed to the arts, especially singing and songwriting.

He helped pass these passions on to his children, and he would later teach Jewel the ins-and-outs of live performance, showing her techniques that she puts into practice to this day. For instance, Atz never performed from a predetermined list of songs, preferring instead to read the audience and respond accordingly. Jewel has carried over that strategy into her own shows, rarely if ever sticking to a set list.

It was Atz who first exposed Jewel to yodeling. A very old form of singing without words, yodeling is characterized by alternating high and low tones. Two examples that you may have heard are "The

Lonely Goatherd" from *The Sound of Music* and the commercial jingle for Swiss Miss instant cocoa. Jewel explained it like this on a Scottish radio program: "You just go from your low voice to your high voice, and as you slide up from your low register to your high register there is a crack."

Yodeling originated in Switzerland, the country where Jewel's grandfather was born. With all but a third of the tiny country consisting of snowcapped mountains, glaciers, forests, and alpine meadows, isolation has always been a factor in the lives of the rural Swiss. Lonely herdsmen developed yodeling as a way to communicate with their fellow mountainfolk. An accomplished yodeler can be heard over great distances.

But it wasn't Yule Kilcher who taught Jewel to yodel. It wasn't even the Swiss who inspired Atz Kilcher to take up this unusual art. Actually it was the American cowboy yodelers of the 1930s and '40s, in particular a bluesman named Jimmie Rodgers.

Jewel has described her childhood as "a science project," referring to the fact that she grew up free of the television and mass media that reflect and reinforce the message that all humans are corrupt. You could also attach the science-project tag to her musical roots, with similarly wonderful results. While most kids were taking megadoses of rock and pop, Jewel's musical youth was spent soaking up the honest sounds of America's Blue Yodeler.

Jewel's career actually echoes that of Jimmie Rodgers. A musical prodigy from an artistic family, he shrugged off the nine-to-five life for the role of traveling troubadour. His first break was a weekly gig on local radio, and he rose from obscurity to release a record in 1928, "Blue Yodel," which sold a million copies, a huge number at that time.

Although he might not be considered one of Jewel's frontline influences, Rodgers was a precursor to Woody Guthrie and Hank Williams, forebears to Bob Dylan who is one of Jewel's musical heroes. In effect, Jewel's yodeling is a tribute to her father, to Jimmie Rodgers, and to those who came before, such as Irish folk singers and Swiss yodelers.

Oddly enough, Jewel's dad was reluctant to teach her how to yodel, saying she was too young. There are people who believe that very young children's vocal chords aren't strong enough for yodeling, and that is often the case.

One thing is certain: her will was plenty strong. She would yodel in bed at night, practicing until she fell asleep. Once, she was even sent home from school with a note from her teacher asking that Jewel stop yodeling during math lessons. It was an early indication of traits that would lead Jewel to fame in later life: insisting on doing what felt right, practicing with zeal, and working outside the status quo.

Jewel's father was also fond of Irish folk music, and Jewel remembers being touched by its beautiful harmonies. The subtle influence of musicians such as the Clancy Brothers can be heard today in the voicings of Jewel's guitar and in the timbre of her vocals.

Not all of Atz's influence on Jewel was musical. He also played a role in teaching her that all people are worthy of equal consideration and basic respect. Jewel reports that her father literally "cried for joy" when, as a teenager, she brought home an African-American boyfriend. He was overjoyed that his daughter had an open mind.

Jewel's parents urged their children to be both open, as in forthcoming and honest, and to be open-minded. They gave their kids extraordinary trust and the freedom to make decisions on their own.

Jewel's mother, Lenedra Carroll (known to most people as Nedra), was an accomplished artist in her own right, a glass sculptor and a fine singer. She worked with Jewel and Jewel's brothers, Shane and little Atz, to develop their appreciation of poetry. She gave them poetry lessons every Monday night and urged them to read and write and sing whenever they felt like doing so.

All three of the Kilcher offspring were raised to become sensitive and artistic: Older brother Shane, now a father himself, works with disabled children, and younger brother Atz travels, plays the harmonica, and writes. Still, it was Jewel who proved to be the extraordinarily gifted and motivated one, willing to explore her creativity in public and practice constantly.

Nedra has always encouraged Jewel to probe her intuitive side and to follow her heart. She cultivated Jewel's love of poetry at the earliest age, and later in life urged her to try mountain retreats, vegetable and juice fasts, and other methods of self-improvement. Much of Jewel's spiritual focus—not to mention her moxie—can be traced to Nedra's guidance and influence.

Nedra and Atz didn't live solely for their cherished progeny; in fact, they both had strong creative drives and were seasoned veterans of public performance. They worked together as a professional singing tandem and even put out a couple of folk albums in the late 1970s: *Early Morning Gold* (1977) and *Born and Raised on Alaskan Land* (1978).

Atz and Nedra eventually incorporated the kids into their stage act, and the family began performing together at dinner shows in area hotels. Jewel's first experiences singing in public came when she was just six years old. The shows consisted of such things as a film of the family's history, the brothers blowing a makeshift horn, short comedic skits, singing by Atz and Nedra, and yodeling by Jewel. The kids were never forced to do anything they didn't want to do, and Jewel looks back with fondness at those exciting and eye-opening days of meeting and singing for apprecia-tive strangers.

Nedra and Atz scheduled gigs almost nightly in the summer months, less often in the winter. During the day Jewel's father was a social worker, while her mother took care of the home and worked on her art.

Everyone recognized that little Jewel was a natural. She wasn't afraid to be in front of crowds, and most important, she simply loved to sing. Atz and Nedra began feeding Jewel a steady diet of new songs and cultivating her musical instincts. She took to the experience like a hummingbird to honeysuckle, and she didn't mind practicing as long and as often as necessary.

Jewel's routine became a feature part of the act, and the local audiences responded with enthusi-asm to the adorable young yodeler. She loved per-forming in front of people, and her charming voice and antics never failed to raise the roof.

Unfortunately, there was more harmony onstage than there was at home between Atz and Nedra; eventually the marriage deteriorated beyond re-pair. Jewel's parents got divorced when she was eight years old. The life that had been romantically rustic—a Little (Alaskan) House on the Prairie—was about to drastically change. "It was like being put underwater," Jewel recalls feeling. But there was nothing that could be done. Nedra needed to get away, "to learn what she needed to learn," as Jewel would later explain in *Request* magazine.

After her mother moved away, Jewel and her brothers stayed in Homer with their dad. Not surprisingly father and daughter didn't always see eye to eye. It was a difficult situation for everyone, but particularly for Jewel, who told *Rolling Stone*, "Leaving your mom on a street corner while you drive away in the back of a car is just . . . brutal. And my dad at that time was out to lunch, bless his heart."

As with most of the experiences in her life, Jewel gleaned wisdom from the painful circumstances, and she now looks back with empathy for her parents. "I learned so much about relationships because I saw both my parents date," she said.

The Kilcher stage show continued as a father-daughter team. They worked the local bars, hotels, and Eskimo villages together for the next several years, with Jewel contributing backup harmonies for her father on a selection of his originals and a variety of covers from many genres—pop, country, folk, and blues.

As she got older it grew clear to Jewel (and everyone else) that she could really sing, not just yodel. She began studying vocalists such as Kate Bush, Jennifer Warnes, Yma Sumac, Nina Simone, and Ella Fitzgerald. She taught herself voice control and also absorbed tremendous songwriting skills that would come into play later in her life.

As for the time she spent performing with her
father, it wasn't all bad . . . but it wasn't all good.
Jewel discovered some sad truths. "You see how
sex becomes a pawn in a chess game. You see it
all," she told *Details* magazine.

As she bloomed into adolescence, Jewel was
sometimes the object of unwanted and illicit attention from men. Thankfully nothing permanently
traumatic happened, and she gained valuable under-
standing about the effects of mixing alcohol and
testosterone.

Jewel strongly asserts that it would be mislead-
ing to portray her childhood as a miserable one—
broken home, nights spent in public houses, that
sort of thing. Most of her early memories are
about eating snow ice cream with fresh blue-
berries, gardening and cutting hay with her father
and brothers, riding horses, and exploring her
artistic impulses.

At least until age eight, Jewel had an idyllic, al-
beit atypical, childhood. She learned to be independent and resourceful, to appreciate the beauty
and solitude of nature, and to make do with just
the bare essentials.

Jewel has always had a rich inner life and a
strong imagination. She recalls that after her parents split, she started writing more poetry as a
method for exploring the intense feelings she
couldn't express out loud. In her words, "That, to

me, is the real beauty of writing: it makes you more intimate with yourself."

It's frustrating for Jewel that her unusual childhood can be portrayed as bleak and unhappy, which is not the way she sees it at all. As she told the *Irish Times*, "Growing up, we all go through a certain amount of pain but my parents gave me the tools to deal with that, as in an open mind. And music, creativity, passion for living, tenacity."

CHAPTER THREE

⌘

A Unique Little Flower

Although she was getting quite a life education outside of school, living on a homestead with three males and singing at nightspots in the evenings, there remained the matter of Jewel's formal education, the history of which is intriguingly diverse.

Jewel's parents made sure she had a head start, planting the seeds of her passion for writing and reading. But there was a period of time in Jewel's early childhood when those two things became very difficult.

Jewel recounted this anecdote—about the first album she ever owned—in the British publication *Mojo*: "I didn't read well when I was about four or five. I listened to every single song on [Pink Floyd's] *The Wall* thinking it was the Pink Panther singing it. . . ."

That's a cute mistake that any young child could

make, but it proved to be indicative of a bigger problem; in fact, Jewel is dyslexic. The simplest definition of dyslexia is "difficulty with language." The word itself comes from the Greek: *dys,* meaning "impaired"; *lexis,* meaning "word." A person who has dyslexia may have problems with any aspect—reading, writing, hearing, speaking—of language.

Researchers and educators don't agree on how much of the population is dyslexic, but the National Institutes of Health estimate the range at 10 to 15 percent. That would mean up to thirty-seven million Americans are affected to varying degrees. Dyslexia is the most common type of learning disability.

Most agree that dyslexia is the culprit when a person struggles to read and/or write despite having normal intelligence, when other factors—physical, emotional, cultural—are not to blame. It cannot be outgrown, but it does not prohibit learning how to learn.

It is not true that all people who have dyslexia "see backward." The condition has nothing to do with vision, although transposition of words and letters does sometimes occur. (Remember the old joke: What does a dyslexic agnostic insomniac do? Stays awake at night wondering if there really is a Dog.)

People with dyslexia are usually male (by an eight-to-one ratio), tend to struggle with subtleties

of language, and often don't read for pleasure—
characteristics that variously either no longer or
never did apply to Jewel. But these same people
can also be highly artistic and tenacious, which are
qualities that Jewel very much does embody. Among
the people who are said to have been dyslexic are
Thomas Edison and Winston Churchill. Jewel is
further proof that dyslexia need not necessarily
hinder success.

Progressing through her early teens, Jewel experimented with different styles as she searched
for her identity. For a while she wore clothes from
the '40s—Coco Chanel imitations and the like.
She joined a rap group, La Creme, the leader of
which was the aforementioned African-American
boyfriend. Jewel's nickname in the group was, ap-
propriately, Swiss Miss.

It was also during this phase of her life, around
ninth grade or so, that Jewel underwent the ritual
from which the "speak from the heart" story in
the prologue of this book is derived. She was unof-
ficially adopted at a powwow by a Native American
family, who told her that she would someday speak
to other people's hearts from her own.

When she was about fifteen years old, Jewel
went to live temporarily with her aunt in Hawaii,
thousands of miles away from home. She had
grown tired of the Alaskan weather, she wasn't

getting along very well with her father, and she wanted to see more of the world.

Made up of eight islands (six of which are open to regular visitors), the fiftieth state is a wondrous world for first-time visitors of any age, especially a perceptive teenager such as Jewel. The dramatic climate, the volcanoes, the tropical landscapes, the expanse of ocean, and the exotic flora and fauna should be seen by everyone at least once in a lifetime. Jewel has said that Hawaii in January is one of the most beautiful places she has ever seen.

Unfortunately, even paradise can't be perfect when it comes to human relations. Jewel's fair skin and blond hair deviated from the norm, and a few of the kids at school didn't immediately welcome the strange face in their midst. "These big Samoan kids wanted to beat me up because I was white . . ." she told *Buzz* magazine. It wasn't the first time that Jewel had seen racial intolerance, but it was the first time she had been the target.

Luckily the ever-resourceful Jewel had a special negotiating chip for bargaining her way out of schoolyard scraps. "I started yodeling—and they just thought it was the coolest thing in the world. After that, they cornered me every day and made me yodel until I was blue in the face." Finding it hard to fit in, Jewel happily waved good-bye to the Aloha State the first chance she got.

She returned to Alaska, still in one piece, to live with her mom in Anchorage, the largest city in the state, with a population of about 225,000. This was her first exposure to urban life, and Anchorage didn't make a particularly favorable impression. Mother and daughter soon relocated south to the city of Seward.

Still itching to stretch her wings, Jewel heard from a friend about a boarding school located in Michigan that was geared toward the training of young artists. "There's always been a bird in me that wanted to fly south. I just didn't know what south was," she has said.

Jewel applied for and was granted a vocal scholarship to attend Interlochen Arts Academy, a prestigious private high school situated between Duck and Green Lakes in northwestern Michigan. Established in 1962 as the nation's first independent high school dedicated to the arts, Interlochen has been home to more Presidential Scholars in the arts than any other high school in the country.

The focus at Interlochen is on individual instruction—the faculty and staff of nearly 300 attend to the education of just 430 students—and the tuition is accordingly expensive. Jewel's scholarship paid only a percentage of her two-year bill, so she raised part of the remainder by putting on a benefit show, with the help of her mom, in Homer. In retrospect, it was Jewel's first solo gig for pay. The rest of the tuition was covered by the income from her summer jobs.

While at Interlochen she started teaching herself to play guitar and write songs, and she began to seriously consider the possibility of pursuing songwriting as a career. Playing guitar was the logical extension of writing poetry and singing, and Jewel had ambitions of traveling the world and being a street musician. Because of her difficulties with learning, she practiced extra hard to get results, but she stuck with it just as she had done with yodeling as a little girl.

In an article written by Richard Gould for *Crescendo*, the official Interlochen newspaper, Jewel's former voice instructor at Interlochen recalled, "What was fun about her was that she was completely game to try anything." Jewel thought she'd be studying the blues at Interlochen, but the instructors wanted her to practice opera. "They asked me to sing an aria and I didn't know what one was," Jewel remembers.

Although she wasn't studying guitar at Interlochen—she is completely self-taught, with the exception of tips that friends have passed on—the artistic environment was an inspiration that drove her to practice as much as she could.

Jewel also wanted to study acting but was told that music majors couldn't attend drama classes. Not one to give up, she begged for an audition and was so impressive that the rule was dropped.

Jewel landed a role in that semester's production of *The Spoon River Anthology*, based on the Edgar Lee Masters collection of free-verse monologues from the graveyard that reveal the secret lives of former residents of a small town. She played an elderly woman.

Jewel has always had strong character and a free spirit, and that came into full bloom at Interlochen. She didn't wear makeup or nail polish, often walked around the campus grounds barefoot, and experimented with spelling her name Juel. "She was a unique little flower," her acting teacher recalls.

Jewel was exploring and learning about herself and others, but she wasn't merely impetuous. On the contrary, her drive and ambition were evident to all her teachers, one of whom commented that "she knew where she was going. Actually, she acted like one of our peers."

To raise extra cash, Jewel modeled for Interlochen sculpture classes. She would even practice her guitar during breaks and make up new poems and songs in her head while she was posing. It was a time when more ideas were bubbling up than she could express, but she was working out the rough sketches of her first songs.

Interlochen expanded Jewel's skills by giving her diverse instruction and creating a practice- and study-intense environment that was brimming with other talented young artists.

She considers her two-year stint there a turning point in her life. "I saw a bigger world. I immersed myself in everything—drama, dance, sculpture, music."

After completing her requirements and performing at the academy's graduation ceremony, Jewel departed Interlochen. The school's most famous alum, Jewel is ironically one of the 5 percent of Interlochen graduates who didn't go on to attend college. Newly come of age, with a heart full of dreams, a head full of ideas, and practically empty pockets, she scraped together money for a train ticket and headed west.

CHAPTER FOUR

San Diego Serenade

Anxious to get on with the rest of her life but unsure of where to begin, Jewel followed the bird that was flying inside her. After making a temporary sojourn through Colorado, she joined Nedra in San Diego.

San Diego isn't an easy city to get a feel for unless you've lived there, but it helps to keep in mind that the area has somewhat of a split personality. The farthest south of the Southern California metropolitan areas, it is located just a few miles north of Tijuana, Mexico, where roughly fourteen million tourists cross the border each year.

The "twin cities" have a complex and somewhat grudging relationship, which is to be expected when a bourgeois American metropolis butts up against a Mexican town where just about every brand of grown-up fun is completely legal.

As social critic Richard Rodriquez once told *The*

Sun magazine: "Of course, San Diego chooses not to regard the two cities as one. Talk about alter ego: Tijuana was created by the lust of San Diego. . . . Tijuana was this lovely meeting of Protestant hypocrisy with Catholic cynicism: the two cities went to bed and both denied it in the morning."

It was here that Nedra, Jewel, and Jewel's younger brother, Atz, rented a house together. Jewel's life during this period was filled with extremes. She had the sunshine, the beaches, chances to meet fun and interesting new people, and the comfort of being near her mom and brother.

On the downside, the three were barely able to make financial ends meet, and the prospects for future earnings were daunting to say the least. Jewel worked at different jobs, answering phones at a computer warehouse and doing some waitressing, but she "basically got fired from all of them" because her heart wasn't in her work. Jewel's life during this time was at once full of promise and dangerously close to chaos.

It has been suggested that living on the edge of chaos is a prerequisite for change, with change being the driving force of life. But to affect real change, an organism (in this case, Jewel) has to take risks that can lead to destruction. Simply put, if your life isn't a little scary, maybe you aren't living to your potential.

"Despite my surroundings, this was a difficult

time for me," Jewel remembers. "I felt a lot of pressure to figure out what I was gonna do with the rest of my life. I was frightened and a little depressed. The idea of spending my life in a nine-to-five job made me feel trapped and hopeless."

It was like being a lab rat in some awful experiment, forced to choose between rent and food each month, with peace of mind hardly an option. She has said of those hand-to-mouth days, "I scraped food off people's plates where I waitressed." There were times when she dated men, her bosses included, simply as a way to get dinner. It was degrading, but playing the game was better than going hungry.

One time Jewel neglected a kidney infection until it became serious, but she wasn't able to afford a doctor, much less the antibiotics she needed. Nedra and Jewel were turned away by several clinics before Jewel finally got help at a hospital. They were living on the edge of chaos and in desperate need of a change.

Jewel was terribly unhappy; not because she didn't want to work hard but because she wasn't doing something that she felt passionate about. The situation was reaching critical mass. It wasn't Jewel's nature to settle into quiet desperation, and she was beginning to wonder whether the life she was living, one without real purpose, was worth continuing.

"I was living entirely without passion and that,

to me, is death," Jewel explained to writer Laura Bond. "I was a terrible waitress, I was a terrible retail salesperson."

At this point most parents probably would have been asserting that their teenage daughter should continue her education; in fact, Jewel's father was urging precisely that course of action. But it wasn't going to happen; Jewel had already made up her mind that she didn't want to go to college.

It was Nedra, who was working part-time at a spa, who suggested that they should move into their respective vehicles and concentrate on pursuing their dreams on an everyday basis. Her influence on Jewel's life at this crucial time was immense, and Nedra has been at her daughter's side, at least in spirit, every step of the way. In the liner notes to *Pieces of You*, Jewel thanked her mom for "teaching me to be a see-er."

Jewel's brother returned to the Homer homestead, where his father and grandfather still lived. As for Jewel, Nedra had always encouraged her to push the boundaries, and it was time for an even more serious leap of faith, one that they would take together.

Jewel has often expressed the belief that instead of being asked "How will you make money?" children should be encouraged to do what they love, thus allowing their passions to blossom into a means of both survival and fulfillment. It's a strategy that certainly worked in Jewel's life, as her childhood love of singing became not just a hobby but a way of life—and a lucrative one at that.

Free from the constraints of toiling at a dead-end job for forty-plus hours a week, Jewel borrowed some money and joyfully took up residence in a blue 1979 Volkswagen van, getting by on a shoestring budget and a steady diet of carrots and peanut butter (which, thanks to Jewel, has become rock 'n' roll's most frequently mentioned food combo since Elvis's banana-and-peanut-butter sandwiches).

No longer a slave to the rent, Jewel spent her days swimming at local beaches, writing poetry at coffee joints, and practicing her guitar. At night she would light candles, read her books, and write. But most of all she meditated on creating a quietude in her life, clearing a path for the things she wanted and the person she was becoming. It was a state of mind she had experienced as a young person in Alaska, and she sought to re-create it in the Golden State.

Jewel and Nedra each had their favorite places to park. Jewel's was next to a small tree with blooming flowers, while her mother's was close to the ocean. Jewel would open the van doors, smell the flowers, and pretend she was back in Alaska.

Not simply mother and daughter but best friends as well, Nedra and Jewel gave each other emotional support. "We would choose sites, park together, open our doors and have tea," Nedra told a *Washington Post* reporter.

Jewel swung from utter desolation to high elation. Her poem "Upon Moving into My Van," found on the inside cover of the *Pieces of You* CD, was written about this period in her life. In it she refers to the "incredible lightness of living" (echoing Milan Kundera's phrase "the unbearable lightness of being," from his book of the same title).

Not that being homeless was a picnic or a lark. Jewel emphasizes that the choice was a financial one; she essentially couldn't afford to eat *and* pay rent. She had to choose, so she opted for transience. From one perspective it was romantic and liberating, but mostly, as Jewel recalls, "It sucked, for sure."

Jewel had taken a deep risk, made a complete commitment to her heart's desire. Now it was time to manifest her dreams into real life or go down trying. Fresh ideas were flowing and her songwriting skills were starting to take shape. She gathered all her energy—the energy she wasn't wasting on a menial job—and focused it on music.

True, she was stealing toilet paper from fast food restaurants, washing her hair in public rest rooms, and taking showers in different friends' apartments, but it seemed an acceptable exchange for the opportunity to devote herself to what she loved. She wasn't thinking about signing a recording contract or going on tour. She just wanted to sing her songs and earn enough cash to live her life.

Of course, practice and preparation are crucial for any performing artist, but perhaps the quickest route to improvement is through "playing out"— in other words, making mistakes in public. This has been an overriding motif throughout Jewel's life and career. She isn't overcome by the fear of taking chances in high-risk situations, no matter who's watching.

Jewel hit the pavement in search of local venues, hoping to earn enough for the bare essentials. Although harboring no illusions about the difficulty of getting started, she was anxious to reach people with her songs.

An extra job she'd had, serving coffee at a place called Java Joe's, proved to be fateful: it was there that Jewel first met Steve Poltz, a local singer-songwriter who had a solo gig at Java Joe's. Steve let Jewel share his stage, and he would go on to help her get introduced and established within the San Diego music scene. He was also instrumental in helping her get a permanent weekly gig.

There are countless legendary bars in the brief history of rock 'n' roll—CBGBs in New York, the Whiskey A Go Go in Los Angeles, the Cavern Club in Liverpool, the list goes on. There have been fewer famous coffeehouses, though several are of no less historical importance: Depression in Calgary (where Joni Mitchell got her start) and Club Mt. Auburn 47 in Cambridge (one of Joan Baez's early haunts), for example.

Enter the Innerchange, the now-defunct java spot where Jewel's career got the lift that propelled her to stardom. Located in the Pacific Beach area, the Innerchange eventually became Jewel's musical home base. The newly opened cafe needed customers and Jewel was in need of listeners. It was a perfect match. By the time Jewel left her last full-time job, she had already begun playing at the Innerchange.

Innerchange owner Nancy Porter recalls, "[Jewel] had just gotten into town, and at the time she was really rough. I knew she'd succeed, I just didn't know it would be to this degree." Porter agreed to let Jewel play every Thursday night at the Innerchange, but things didn't go so well at first.

Like any fledgling artist Jewel did her own promotion, which meant passing out flyers. She received several unwanted offers from men on the street, but people were generally unresponsive to the prospect of going to see an unknown songwriter perform.

When the night of that first show arrived, the crowd was far from capacity. "I showed up to my gig hoping some people would be there and there was probably about six and it broke my heart," Jewel remembers.

It was an ego-deflating experience, and it was

also worrisome in terms of basic survival. Jewel's pay was coming from the three-dollar admission charge, and she hoped to at least collect enough for gasoline and food to last through the week.

As showtime approached, tears were on the verge of flowing, but she went outside, took a deep breath, and pulled herself together. Once she got onstage Jewel found that the people who were lucky enough to witness her first Thursday night show at the Innerchange responded with kindness and enthusiasm. Her spirits lifted and she finished the show, then thanked everyone in attendance one by one.

After making an extended visit back to Homer and celebrating her nineteenth birthday, Jewel returned to San Diego and picked up the pace.

At various times in this phase of her life, Jewel sporadically appeared at local bars—the Belly Up, the Green Circle, the Live Wire—and other area coffeehouses, such as Java Joe's. She also went for an audition at a coffee shop called Cafe Crema but was turned down.

From late 1993 Jewel performed almost exclusively at the Innerchange for regular Thursday night sessions until being discovered by the record companies in early 1994. Jewel played her final show at the Innerchange in early 1995.

During those salad days (". . . when I was green in judgment," wrote Shakespeare) at the Inner-change, Jewel flashed the spark of what has become her performance trademark: spontaneity. But her act was considerably less polished.

Like most inexperienced musicians, she tended to take a lot of time between songs, showing frustration when her guitar wouldn't stay in tune or when the guitar picks, which were often borrowed from audience members, weren't to her liking.

She frequently played songs she had recently written without having ironed out the kinks, and it wasn't uncommon for her to forget her own lyrics and chord progressions. Actually, these are things she still does to this day, which brings up a rather fascinating facet of Jewel's character and style—the ability to turn minor, so-called imperfections into virtues.

Touring the nightspots of Alaska with her father, Jewel had learned that putting on a great show means reaching out to bridge the gap between artist and audience. Since her innate impulse is to connect with people in everyday life, she's a natural at doing it on the stage.

Improvisation is key, and nothing says spontaneity like an imperfect—in other words, unrehearsed—moment. It isn't that Jewel fakes mistakes, but she also doesn't panic when they occur; in fact, she turns them to her advantage. As was the case with the Grateful Dead, for example, the screwups make the triumphs feel that much more genuine.

In the beginning, Jewel sometimes felt insecure about how the audience would react to deeply emotional songs such as "Don't," which is about the vulnerability felt when one is in love. She had to teach herself to make eye contact and trust that people would be compelled to give their full attention. Her stage presence was getting stronger with every performance.

Jewel's self-deprecating remarks set the crowds at ease. She told jokes and funny stories, bantered with audience members, and delivered hours of original songs, in addition to the occasional cover of Tracy Chapman's "Behind the Wall," an a cappella song about domestic violence.

Quirky and unassuming, Jewel's natural inclination to connect with the audience went beyond merely singing onstage. At the end of every set, Jewel would hurry to the front door, shake hands with people, and thank each of them for coming.

It's next to impossible for a musician to fake her feelings in such an intimate setting as the small, dark Innerchange. Jewel's sincerity proved to be as much of an asset as her incredible voice. Listeners couldn't help but be touched, and they invariably brought friends with them the following Thursday.

The Innerchange shows, especially in the middle period when the buzz was high but the crowds hadn't grown overwhelming, were like weekly family reunion parties, with fans bringing food from home so that Jewel would be adequately fed until the next show.

Over the months word spread. It wasn't long before the admission price was up to five bucks and latecomers were being turned away at the door. Jewel was doing two shows per night, and the crowds were so thick that she had to walk across the tables to reach the stage.

The local music press was stirring up interest. *Slamm* magazine raved, "Her voice is many things, all of them beautiful. When she opens up, the sound is crystalline and pure." Area acoustic musicians were turning up most every week to join Jewel on-stage. Foremost among them were members of the Rugburns, Gregory Page and Rob "Doc" Driscoll (who have since left the band) and Steve Poltz.

San Diego is known more for its surfers, its zoo, and its retirees than for having a burgeoning music scene. But while it has yet to emerge on the level of Austin, Seattle, New York, or Los Angeles, the San Diego scene is unique because it is predominantly acoustic (with notable exceptions such as Rocket from the Crypt).

There are numerous local acoustic acts that could get increased attention in the wake of Jewel's success: Holly Bell, Mary Dolan, John Katchur, Steve Dehyes, Christopher Prim, Don Everett Pearce, and Steve Harris, to name a few. They all have unique traits and talents and are worth checking out.

One of San Diego's most popular local acts is the Rugburns, whose cofounder and frontman, the aforementioned Steve Poltz, is Jewel's longtime confidant, frequent songwriting collaborator, and former boyfriend. There were some locals who called Jewel and Steve the Evan Dando and Juliana Hatfield of San Diego, in reference to a speculated romance between the two East Coast alternarockers.

Steve cowrote two songs on what would become Jewel's debut CD, including the smash single "You Were Meant for Me." She has noted that one of her favorites of the songs that they wrote together is "I Drove by My Old Lover's Mother's House," which starts delicate and lovely, then closes with wailing sonic fireworks. Jewel has said of Steve, "He's really pushed me as a songwriter to demand a lot of myself."

One of the best songs that Jewel and Steve wrote together is "Food Stamp Love," which they sometimes play together in concert. It's about being with a person who only wants to dole out small portions of love, and is written from the point of view of someone for whom that isn't enough.

The Rugburns were the opening act for many dates on Jewel's first American tour, and they've joined her onstage as a backing band countless times. Jewel has also turned up at Rugburns gigs on occasion. Not surprisingly, Jewel has called the Rugburns her favorite band and Steve "the best songwriter."

The band's output is a fluid hybrid of folk, punk, country-western, and the odd show tune. They combine often irreverent lyrics with crisp hooks and frenetic energy, and they are superb players. The Rugburns, who have existed as such since approximately 1988, were a quartet before co-founder Rob Driscoll dropped out; Steve Poltz remains the driving force behind the band.

In the tradition of Jimmy Buffet's "My Head Hurts, My Feet Stink, and I Don't Love Jesus," the Rugburns should probably win an arbitrary award for funniest song titles, with "Why Are You Going Out with That Gold's Gym Guy" at the head of the pack, closely followed by "Baby, I'm Going to Have to Give You Up for Lent," and "My Whole Purpose on Earth Is Just to Kiss Your Ass." Jewel helped create that last one, and she occasionally performs it in concert.

Steve, who has been known to wear a dress (he's a dreamboat in taffeta) and is not above flashing his backside for the audience's amusement, also has a knack for writing more serious, introspective songs. As he told *Addicted to Noise* reporter Gil Kauffman, "I've made peace with the quid pro quo aspect of playing these jokier songs along with the more sober ones about my problems with intimacy and my tales of heartbreak."

Steve is like the little kid whose teacher tells him not to run with a sharp object in his mouth. But the sharp object is his tongue, and it seems to be stuck permanently in his cheek. Jewel credits

Steve for helping her develop a fuller appreciation for humor in music.

It's easy to see why they made for such an interesting couple back then and why they still get along so well. Although no longer linked romantically, Jewel and Steve remain close friends and songwriting partners (the credits Wiggly Tooth and Polio Boy on the copyright line from *Pieces of You* refer to Jewel and Steve).

They make impromptu appearances at each other's concerts; for instance, when the Rugburns played at the Belly Up in Solana Beach, San Diego, just before Christmas 1997, Jewel made a surprise showing. Wearing a cowboy hat and jeans, Jewel joined Steve in performing a set of five songs they've written together, including "You Were Meant for Me." The Rugburns accompanied Jewel when she sang one of her own songs, "Who Will Save Your Soul."

Jewel and the Rugburns also hooked up New Year's Eve 1997 at the Hard Rock Cafe in Las Vegas. Ticket prices were in the $150 range, a far cry from the halcyon days of three-dollar shows at the Innerchange.

The Rugburns have two full-length CDs, *Morning Wood* and *Taking the World by Donkey*, plus an EP called *Mommy I'm Sorry*. Their rarely seen video for the song "Hitchhiker Joe" features an appearance by Jewel (in the role of Steve's girlfriend).

Mercury Records has released a Steve Poltz solo

disc, and the final track selections include three tunes cowritten by Jewel: "Impala," "I Thought I Saw You Last Night," and "Silver Lining." The CD is titled *One Left Shoe*.

The Rugburns are still together as a band and should be putting out a new CD in 1998. If you want to get a feel for what flips Jewel's skirt, musically speaking, checking out the Rugburns is a must.

CHAPTER FIVE

❧

Discovered

As crowds at the Innerchange continued to swell, news flowed up the Pacific Coast to Los Angeles–based record companies that a brilliant young songwriter was making waves in San Diego. Word was she had the best voice, male or female, that anyone in San Diego had heard since Eddie Vedder left for Seattle to front Pearl Jam.

Jewel still didn't have much cash flow, but her Thursday shows at the Innerchange had become standing-room-only events, while her days were filled with poetry, surfing, and contemplation. It felt the way she imagined Paris in the 1920s might have been—minus the surfing.

Record executives began making the two-hour trip down Highway 5 to see Jewel at the Innerchange. Blown away by what they heard and saw, the A&R reps knew that they could be witnessing the start of a magical success story. Jewel's fans and friends knew it, too, and they let the people from the record companies know exactly how much they loved Jewel and her music.

In fact, Jewel was about to begin living a true Cinderella existence. One night she'd be whisked away to luxury hotels and four-star dinners, and the next day she'd be back in her blue van eating that fabled combo of carrots and peanut butter.

Jewel had never seriously considered the idea that she would get a recording contract so quickly, if ever. Now it seemed her fairy-tale dream was about to reach a happy pinnacle. What remained to be seen was which company would have a hand in putting the glass slipper on Jewel's foot.

Every music publisher employs A&R (Artist & Repertoire) representatives. They serve as talent scouts, listening for news of undiscovered performers and traveling where the scuttlebutt takes them. These are the first industry insiders an artist must impress to have any hope of making it in the music business.

At one point, Jewel was visited by an A&R rep from Virgin Records. Refreshingly unpretentious, she was thrilled by the attention. "I bought him a burrito; he told me I could make a record," she said later in an interview with *LAUNCHonline*. Other reps soon followed, presenting Jewel with a choice regarding which company should shepherd her fledgling career.

In early 1994 an A&R rep named Jenny Price,

working for Atlantic Records (she has since moved
on to Mercury), came to see Jewel at the Innerchange. Price loved what she saw. Following a
brief period of negotiation—under the guidance of
Inga Vainshtein, who is now Jewel's comanager
with Nedra—Jewel joined the fold of artists at
Atlantic. It had taken just about five months for
Jewel to go from unknown to under contract.
Jewel used her advance to buy a used Volvo and a
new guitar.

A month later Jewel was flying to New York,
all expenses paid, for a showcase concert that
had been arranged for the employees of Atlantic
Records. The event was held at Film Center Cafe
on the west side of Manhattan. Jewel performed
brilliantly, and when the final note had died away,
she had won over the entire audience. Danny
Goldberg, who is now the chief of Warner Bros.
Records, said, "It amazed me that someone so
young could sing with so much conviction. It was
inspiring."

Even though the showcase wasn't a publicized
appearance for a cheering crowd of thousands, this
was a special night for Jewel. Being discovered,
signed, and recorded is only part of the star-
making process; Jewel actually had to be "promoted" to the higher-ups at Atlantic so that they
would focus their huge financial resources on her.
It was essential for Jewel to capture the attention

and devotion of important people along the chain of command who would help champion her music.

One such person was Ron Shapiro, who became general manager/senior vice president at Atlantic at about the time *Pieces of You* was released. At every sales and marketing meeting, he pushed the idea that Jewel was headed for stardom if given proper support. His conviction and loyalty were essential because, in the end, Jewel's debut CD required an extraordinary amount of time to break into the mainstream.

"At a lot of companies, Jewel would have been over a long time ago," Shapiro told *Rolling Stone* when *Pieces of You* finally began to take off about a year and a half after it hit the stores. But having faith in Jewel and her debut CD would eventually pay off, both for her and for Atlantic.

It's fascinating that even Jewel, with her special talent, needed to curry the support of key executives within her own record label. Only then could she reach the listeners who would eventually buy her CDs. Bottom line: it takes more than just great songs to make a superstar. It takes a strong network of support within the record company.

After the Film Center Cafe showcase, Jewel took up a residency at Ludlow Cafe, a very small spot on New York's Lower East Side. The first week, there were only a couple of Atlantic employees on hand, but by the end of the month there were many more. All were duly impressed with

Jewel, and she was equally so with them. "You know the stories about the record-company bad guys?" Jewel asked in *Billboard* magazine. "It hasn't been true at Atlantic. They're good people, and they manage to do their business and care about music, too."

Some of the performers on the Atlantic imprint have included Led Zeppelin, Phil Collins, Foreigner, Hootie & The Blowfish, and many more of the most popular and influential rock acts in music history. The label recently celebrated its golden anniversary. When a company with that much history behind it decides to sign and promote an artist, you might think that the hits would fall into place with a snap of the fingers.

Not necessarily. Atlantic, which is owned by Time Warner, has been arguably the top pop-music label the past couple of years by breaking artists, such as Tori Amos, Duncan Sheik, and Jewel, who at first glance didn't appear headed for big sales.

The driving force behind the company is the cochairman and coCEO team of Ahmet Ertegun, who founded the company in 1948, and Val Azzoli, who joined Atlantic in 1990. Azzoli is best known in the industry for having been general manager at SRO during the years when Canadian progressive rockers Rush broke through to sell millions of records despite little radio airplay. That scenario rings familiar with regard to Jewel, whose songs were at first considered "unlistenable" and "unplayable" by the mainstream radio stations and music video networks.

There was no question that Jewel had the talent to be a star, but it wasn't going to happen without patience, a rarity in the record business. Thankfully, the people at Atlantic believed in Jewel and were willing to wait for the world to catch on. Their thinking was that with her potential for broad appeal, Jewel would be best served by getting promotional boosts in different markets, from college radio to modern adult contemporary stations.

It's a fact of life in the industry that if an artist becomes identified exclusively with one type of listener, an entire demographic can be lost. The reps planned to break Jewel with young listeners first, reasoning that she'd have immediate appeal among her peers. Atlantic sent out promotional CDs to college radio stations; in fact, the first record chart on which Jewel appeared was for *College Music Journal*.

At this stage of her career Jewel had a loyal San Diego following and the backing of her record company, but commercial radio and video networks ridiculed the concept of putting a solo female folksinger on the air. It was up to Jewel to hit the road and develop a national fan base at the grassroots level.

And that's exactly what she did in her own unique way.

CHAPTER SIX

Making *Pieces*

It happens that in the labyrinth of the corporate music world, the voices of the A&R people "on the street" may not be heard in the offices of the executives who decide how an artist will be marketed. Big decisions needed to be made regarding how Jewel would be promoted to the public, and they needed to be the right ones if her music was going to reach the audience it deserved. Thankfully the proposed strategy of Jenny Price, the A&R rep who signed Jewel, and Inga Vainshtein, Jewel's comanager, was heard and heeded.

Their idea was to let Jewel's audience grow "organically." She would play for as many people in as many cities as possible, with "Jewel introducing herself to the public and people discovering her naturally," as Price explained.

Atlantic would arrange (and pick up the comparatively small tab) for Jewel to be on the road almost constantly. She would drive herself in a rental car, perform at a high school during the day, open for a headliner in the evening, then finish at a coffeehouse or bar later the same night.

In this way Jewel could reach a large and diverse network of potential fans, who would discover her and tell their friends. As her reputation grew, it wouldn't be long before radio stations and record stores across every region of the country would be deluged with requests for Jewel's music.

But first things must come first. Before she could set out to meet the rest of America, Jewel needed to record her first official CD. And before she could do that, a producer needed to be chosen, one who could help capture the authentic Jewel sound at that early phase of her musical development.

The role of a music producer isn't easy to define, but it is roughly parallel to that of a movie director in so much as a movie director determines what you see on screen, while a music producer influences what you hear on a CD. Generally speaking, the idea is to help clarify the artist's vision and let it shine through.

(By the way, if you are a young woman interested in being part of the female revolution in music, studying to be a producer or engineer would be a fine route to take. The profession remains male dominated at the moment, even as women are making inroads onstage.)

There was a lot of discussion about who would supervise the production on Jewel's debut CD. "We wanted to make an honest and pure record with mainly just her and the guitar," Jenny Price explained.

The idea was to keep the sound as natural as possible—thereby encapsulating the intimacy of Jewel's performances—so getting the right person was essential. After working through dozens of options, Jewel was finally introduced to a man named Ben Keith.

Although you've probably never heard of him, there's a good chance you know Ben Keith's work. When he was only sixteen years old, he played steel guitar for country music legend Patsy Cline on her classic "I Fall to Pieces." He also performed on Neil Young's biggest-selling release, *Harvest,* in 1972, and he coproduced Neil's *Harvest Moon* twenty years later.

Jewel decided right away that Ben was the perfect person to produce her first CD. She wanted to document where she was as a young musician, and that required a producer who knew how to create a comfortable environment for Jewel's first experience in a studio.

Jewel said of her relatively unharnessed talent, "It's kind of like new grass—walk on it too much and it's killed." She wanted a producer who would enhance her songs while sticking to the basics, and she found that person in Ben Keith.

The process of recording in a studio is usually more difficult than performing in front of an audience. The artist knows that a CD is a permanent record and understandably wants it to be free of mistakes. But it's difficult to relax and get in the groove when you're trying to play flawlessly. The more you fret about perfection, the harder it is to attain. "It's hard for me doing it in the studio with no one around," Jewel told *The Island Ear*. "It's like trying to fake an orgasm or something."

With her history of singing in public as a child, then doing shows at bars and coffee shops as a young adult, Jewel is foremost a live performer, so it made sense to record most of her debut CD in front of a live audience. And where better to do that than at the Innerchange, the San Diego coffeehouse where she'd gotten her big break.

Jewel played shows over the course of two nights from which the live songs on *Pieces of You* were culled. Admission was first come first seated, with an eight-dollar price tag. Whatever had been planned going in, the final choice for which songs to play belonged to Jewel. "She is her own person and she plays whatever she feels like playing," said Jenny Price.

Songs not chosen from the Innerchange tapings would be taken from sessions done a month later in Neil Young's Redwood Digital Facility at Broken Arrow Ranch in Woodside, California.

The plan was to avoid studio slickness. Keep it simple, keep it real, and allow Jewel's natural soulfulness to hit the listeners right in the heart. The style of production on Neil Young's records were the model, which is one of the major reasons that Young's cohort, Ben Keith, was selected to captain the recording process. Jewel, too, put a great deal of input into the production of *Pieces of You*.

With the exception of "Who Will Save Your Soul," most of the songs give only the slightest hint that musicians other than Jewel were involved. That particular track, which is the all-important leadoff, features the Stray Gators, one of Neil Young's backing bands. The musicians are Spooner Oldman (who got his nickname because he "dished out his eye with a spoon") on keyboards, Tim Drummond on bass, and Oscar Butterworth (who charmed Jewel with stories of his days with Bob Dylan and even compared Jewel to Janis Joplin) on drums.

It was more than a little intimidating for Jewel to be playing alongside such old pros. But the Stray Gators did their best to make Jewel feel at home, and it turned out to be a priceless experience for both her and Steve Poltz, who was also present for much of the process.

Perhaps the most exciting moment in the studio came when Jewel was working on "Don't." She was playing an old Martin brand guitar that had an incredibly warm tone. When she asked about the instrument's origins, she was told that it had once belonged to Hank Williams, the most influential country-western songwriter who ever lived. "I just sat there and tried to vibe in the energy," Jewel enthused.

A few of the pieces that were expected to be among the chosen cuts were eventually bumped out of the mix. Some of the less obvious options were included due to how well Jewel had performed them at the Innerchange tapings. For example, "I'm Sensitive" was written just before the Innerchange recordings were done and certainly wasn't expected to be among the final picks. And Jenny Price notes, "I can't say from the demo that 'Who Will Save Your Soul' was an obvious single, but it just came out great. . . ."

There were some very hard choices to make in cutting *Pieces of You* to its eventual fourteen-song, fifty-nine-minute running time. As for the songs that did make the cut, every one is a priceless gem.

CHAPTER SEVEN

Looking at *Pieces*

"The most punk-rock thing you could do
now is make a folk record."
—Rick Rubin, record producer
(Def Jam), 1995

Jewel's stunning debut, *Pieces of You*, has spent well over 100 weeks—and counting—on *Billboard*'s chart of the top CDs. It peaked at number 4 and was still in the top 25 in late January 1998. It ranked as the number 2 bestselling CD of 1997, despite having been released back on February 28, 1995. It was certified Platinum (one million copies sold) on August 6, 1996.

A double-LP, vinyl-only version was released in 1997. It included five extra tracks: "Emily," "Rocker Girl," "Everything Breaks Sometimes," "Cold Song," and "Angel Needs a Ride."

Jon Matsumoto, writing in the *Los Angeles Times*, commented, "On her debut album, *Pieces of You*, singer-songwriter Jewel challenges listeners with darkly shaded acoustic material that is lyrically complex and compassionately executed. . . ."

A review in *Time Out* magazine called it "[A] haunting work of pain and beauty from an artist whose style is stark and honest, and whose songs are deftly observed and deeply compelling."

Jewel has commented, looking back on her debut CD, "I don't think [*Pieces of You*] is a great album. . . . But it's got a lot of heart." That statement may not fully represent how Jewel feels about her first recorded effort, but it is indicative of the fact that she frequently seems torn between acknowledging its faults and sticking up for what she rightfully believes, track by track, is an exceptional first release that stands on its own merits.

Who Will Save Your Soul

With an upbeat, full-band arrangement, this song is perhaps the least characteristic of the overall musical style of *Pieces of You*. The rhythm section of Tim Drummond (bass) and Oscar Butterworth (drums) lays down a strong groove in back of Jewel's no-nonsense lyrics. "Who Will Save Your Soul" is an indictment of modern urban life and an open challenge for listeners to take responsibility for their own salvation, rather than looking to outside sources.

She wrote the song at age seventeen, but there are conflicting stories about where she wrote it (either on a long bus ride or the lawn of a schoolyard) and the source of inspiration (meeting a young man in Los Angeles who had never walked on grass in his bare feet and/or seeing people in Mexico who thought that America, as shown on TV, was the promised land). Jewel has often lamented that the media distorts reality by sending the message that people are corrupt, and that people then act out a self-fulfilling prophecy.

This was the first single from *Pieces of You*, and it peaked at number 11 on *Billboard*'s Hot 100 chart. It has also appeared on at least five Atlantic Records promotional releases, and a live version—featuring bass work by Flea of the Red Hot Chili Peppers—is available on the compilation *Live on Letterman: Music from the Late Show*.

Pieces of You

The title track is deceptively catchy—you find yourself happily humming the tune in spite of the darkly intense lyrics. Jewel herself has said that she thought everyone would hate it, but *Addicted to Noise* called it "the disc's strongest song, as honest as it is somber."

Jewel has said that she originally wrote the song about a girl who hated her (she even considered calling it "Ugly Girl"), but she takes it beyond the personal and into an unflinching indictment of bigotry and hatred in general.

She told *Stereotype* magazine, "I think the more confident and secure we are with ourselves, the less judgmental we are with other people. It's ultimately a song that urges people to be kind to one another."

Little Sister

Like the track that comes before it, this song looks into the dark corners of human behavior. The enemies here are all forms of addiction and the starvation of the soul that goes with them.

Songwriters try to integrate the music and the lyrics so that the song feels complete, and Jewel succeeds in that endeavor here with a happy-go-lucky melody that calls to mind a young girl skipping lightly toward an uncertain fate.

This is one of the first songs Jewel wrote. She doesn't have a sister; the words refer to an old friend's younger brother. Jewel explains, "It made me sad to see there was so much beauty around and all he could think to do was drugs and TV."

Jewel almost never talks about the song without mentioning television, a perspective that echoes the words of U.S. Congresswoman Shirley Chisolm, who in 1969 said: "It is not heroin or cocaine that makes one an addict. It is the need to escape from a harsh reality. There are more television addicts . . . in this country than there are narcotics addicts."

"Little Sister" is one of Jewel's most misunderstood songs.

Foolish Games

The third single from *Pieces of You*, "Foolish Games" spurred a resurgence in sales of Jewel's debut CD, which in turn caused further delay in the production of a follow-up. (Record companies understandably avoid issuing new releases until the current material has run its course.) "I pray to God there will be no more singles. I'm gonna be twenty-five before my next album comes out," she told an MTV reporter.

One of the most emotional, tragic, romantic songs to hit the pop charts in years, it seems to strike a chord with everyone who hears it. Take a walk around a store where "Foolish Games" is coming through the sound system. You're likely see everyone from Latino teenagers to Ukrainian grandmothers singing along—with feeling.

A double A-side (backed with "You Were Meant for Me"), it finished as 1997's second-bestselling single. A rerecorded version, arguably even more powerful than the one on *Pieces of You*, can be found on the *Batman & Robin* soundtrack, although it wasn't in the film itself.

Jewel says that she pieced together "Foolish Games" from short poetic verses she had written over the years. She then added the chorus to connect the verses. Charlotte Caffrey, formerly of 1980s group the Go Gos, contributes magnificently on piano. "Foolish Games" is reminiscent of Kate Bush's highly emotional and operatic compositions.

Near You Always

Jewel has talked about this song as if it were visited upon her rather than created by her, saying, "It just wouldn't let me go to sleep one night till it was four A.M. and finished." In a stream of pure feeling, "Near You Always" embodies the fear and desire that come with putting your heart in another person's control.

Jewel has been known to open her live shows by singing this song a cappella. The line "Your hands are in my hair, but my heart is in your teeth" says it all.

Painters

In this song, Jewel stretches her imagination ahead a few decades to write about the feelings of an elderly woman whose husband has passed away. As she looks back on their life together as artists, she reflects on the possibility of immortality through art and the interweaving of beauty and art in everyday life. In effect, the characters have "painted" their lives together.

This song also appeared on a hard-to-find demo cassette called *Shiva Diva Doo Wop* that Jewel made prior to the release of *Pieces of You*.

Morning Song

A sweet, endearing look at a happy couple with nothing to do in the morning but enjoy each other's company, this is probably the disc's most lighthearted entry. Notice the playful sexiness in Jewel's voice when she sings the line "I'm gonna give you some more."

Piano coloring by Robbie Buchanon and the smooth bass notes of Mark Howard weave a delicate tapestry. The result is a pop-country treasure that stands alongside the Velvet Underground's "Sunday Morning" as one of the best prebreakfast tunes ever written.

Adrian

Clocking in at 7:02, "Adrian" is the longest track on *Pieces of You*. The story is a made-up one—Jewel didn't know anyone named Adrian, and the only Mary Epperson she knows was a piano teacher in Homer, Alaska.

The story is about a boy who suffers severe brain damage in a canoe accident and the friend who remains loyal to his memory. This is one of the two songs on the CD that were cowritten with Steve Poltz. Jewel has called the song "an experiment," and some critics were less than kind to the results.

I'm Sensitive

The newest of the songs included on *Pieces of You*, Jewel says that it has at least two things in common with the title track: it was written very quickly in a state of high emotion, and she thought that everyone would hate it. Actually, it's one of the CD's most poignant songs.

The most autobiographical of the tracks on *Pieces of You*, it is anything but the feeble plea for delicacy that a superficial listen might imply. This is Jewel's "Get Off of My Cloud," only without the shouting. The harmony vocals in the chorus are pretty as can be, but the sentiments are strong and raw. It has been suggested that there may be slight warbles in the repeating guitar line, but if the song isn't polished to a glossy perfection, that only adds to its honest charm.

The song also turns up on a couple of Atlantic promotional discs, including two versions on *Save the Linoleum*. As she explains in the introduction to the live version, Jewel believes that if people are surrounded by beauty, they become beautiful. She also recognizes that the inverse is true, and there is a wise element of personal vulnerability in her words and intonations. She's aware of the potential for cynicism in a world that doesn't value sensitivity. As she says, "Innocence isn't really ever lost, we just need to maintain it."

"I'm Sensitive" contains the line "We are everyday angels" from which Jewel's fans, The Everyday Angels, take their name.

You Were Meant for Me

As a double A-side with "Foolish Games," this proved to be one of the biggest-selling singles of 1997. A song about the feelings that are left behind when a loved one leaves, and the way everyday actions and objects can make us sad by reminding us of what used to be, it could be called the mournful side of "Morning Song."

Jewel has jokingly said that she wrote "You

Were Meant for Me" with Steve Poltz while "on a three-day research project . . . the point of which being to determine whether or not spaghetti squash would feel like fur if you felt it with your left hand while petting a pigmy pig with your right."

This is another track that features the Stray Gators; drummer Oscar Butterworth chips in fine brushwork and soft yet dramatic cymbal accents.

The song was also included on several Atlantic promos in different versions, such as an acoustic duet with Steve Poltz and a remix by Juan Patiño. Asked why the version heard on the radio differs from the one on *Pieces of You*, Jewel replied, "because I can't stand my singing on the album version. Plus, it is always fun to try something new."

Don't

Probably the oldest of the songs on *Pieces of You*, "Don't" was one of the first songs Jewel wrote. It has been known to make listeners cry, especially when played back-to-back with the non–*Pieces of You* track "1,000 Miles Away." A lyrical cousin to "Near You Always," it looks at the vulnerability of a person who is in love with someone who isn't right for her. The speaker implores the one she loves to not use the power he has over her.

Jewel has explained that she originally struggled with the time signature, playing the guitar part in

4/4 while singing in 3/4, a feat that could cause brain damage if done too often. It may have been an ugly baby when first conceived, but it grew into a real knockout. The delicate, waltzlike guitar part suggests a Chopin nocturne, while the plaintive, halting lyrical delivery will break your heart if you've got one and show you what you're missing if you don't. Jewel draws out the notes near the end for extra emotional effect.

This is another tune that Jewel guessed would fall flat. "I thought it was the dumbest song I ever wrote and I wouldn't play it for anybody," she told radio DJ Mike Halloran.

Daddy

As everyone hopefully knows by now, this song isn't about Jewel's father. With the exception of one line, "Daddy" comes across as a fierce look at the effects of past child abuse on a sensitive young adult. A passing reference to the Ku Klux Klan lends the only clue to the song's origin, a childhood incident in which a friend's father admonished his children for watching black people on TV, specifically *The Jeffersons*.

Angel Standing By

This song is a musical tribute to heaven-sent souls that many people believe watch over and protect us. For those who aren't inclined to trust in the existence of literal angels, the song can be enjoyed as a simple, heartfelt pledge by one loved one to another. In any case, the dreamy vocals were definitely sent from a better world.

Amen

Of all the songs she has written, Jewel has said that this one is her personal favorite. With words that tap into our collective unconscious, she delves into the price of fame, the death of idols, and the hopelessness felt by many fans after Nirvana frontman Kurt Cobain's suicide. Jewel has ended countless concerts with a chicken-skin inducing rendition of "Amen."

The following five songs were included on the 1997 double-album release of *Pieces of You*:

Emily

A brutally sad song, "Emily" explores the "death of a child" theme from *The Crossing Guard*, the film for which it was written. The vocal line starts quiet and broken, but along the way we hear Jewel test the deep end of her range. She also adds some lovely harmonizing. The barely existent guitar line is an ideal complement to the lyrics; it feels as if Jewel is about to fade into nothingness out of sheer grief.

Rocker Girl

It's short and acoustic and thoroughly Jewel, but "Rocker Girl" could just as easily have been a '80s-girl-group tribute or a singalong from the movie *Grease*. A funny paean to white trash kids reminiscent of Bait-N-Tackl's raucous classic "Trailer Park Girl," Jewel's "Rocker Girl" somehow manages to draw a romantic link between blue eyeliner and black eyes. The joyfully campy boppin'-down-the-street guitar lines show how masterful Jewel is at linking her music and words into pristine pop nuggets.

Everything Breaks Sometimes

This is a harsh breakup song, like "Sometimes It Be That Way," except without the humorous detachment or the peppy feel. It takes a while for the guitar hook to sink in, but when it does you can't shake it.

Jewel will explore emotions from every vantage point, so many of her lyrical motifs echo through more than one song. "Everything Breaks Sometimes" is a look at what happens when you're left trying to apologize for the way life goes.

Cold Song

Jewel supposedly conceived "Cold Song" in her sleep and wrote it while traveling to Toronto. It's definitely a crowd pleaser on par with "I Hate Valentine's Day," another one of her flights of whimsy that, too, is very funny and far too brief. Bouncy and country-tinged, "Cold Song" delves into how the bond of love can be strengthened by a runny nose. A bit like "Morning Song," with its call-in-sick-and-stay-in-bed theme, "Cold Song" closes with a tongue-twister-in-cheeky proposition: "Do you wanna wanna do me."

Angel Needs a Ride

This is a tribute to a long-lost friend, as well as a terrific road song about sad souls searching for solace on a lost highway. It could easily have been the theme song to the film *Leaving Las Vegas*. "Angel Needs a Ride" is one of the most-referenced and best-known of Jewel's songs that weren't originally included on *Pieces of You*. It's one of the first tunes she recorded and remains a very popular part of her concert repertoire.

It also became something of a rallying cry—in the same way that "I need a miracle" was for ticketless Deadheads—for the fans who were in need of transport to the 1996 concert known as "Jewelstock."

CHAPTER EIGHT

Pieces Releases

March 2, 1995, was a historic day for Jewel, for Atlantic, and for the San Diego music scene. That was the date of Jewel's first CD release concert and party. *Pieces of You* had hit the stores a couple of days earlier.

In the morning Jewel did an in-studio interview at TV station KUSI in San Diego. She also performed "501 Beauty Queen" on the air. In the evening she performed two shows at the Hahn Cosmopolitan Theater. The atmosphere was electric as Jewel's old friends from the Innerchange mingled with her new supporters.

Before the start of the second set, Jewel told the audience, "You know I still haven't been sponsored," a reference to the early days at the Innerchange, when she used to make jokes about getting a corporate sponsorship for the bottled water she constantly consumed.

She was in brilliant voice throughout both shows, letting it all hang out on songs from hot-off-the-press *Pieces of You*. She also did other tunes, both old and new, such as "Perfectly Clear" and "Swedish Lullaby." She also played a few tunes with the Rugburns, flashing her rockin' side on "God's Gift to Women," in addition to delving into the more sensitive of her collaborations with Steve Poltz on acoustic songs such as "Silver Lining."

Jewel closed the set alone onstage with a devastating version of "Amen," and the crowd showed how much they loved her with a lengthy standing ovation. Not yet accustomed to the acclaim, Jewel exclaimed, "Stop it, guys, you're embarrassing me!" It was something she would be reliving often in the days, months, and years to come.

The event was covered by all the local news stations, complete with interviews and footage. Jewel had all of San Diego's fondest wishes, but she also had a long and winding road ahead of her.

The title "Hardest Working Man in Music" has been used to describe such giants as soul demigod James Brown and blue-collar rocker Bruce Springsteen. Jewel may not be in a league with such legends in terms of longevity, but in the three years that followed the release of *Pieces of You*, she was arguably the hardest-working performer in the industry.

Her tireless efforts in promoting *Pieces of You* often included doing several interviews and three shows each and every day for months at a stretch. It wasn't uncommon for her to work as many as forty cities in thirty days, a grinding workload even for a seasoned veteran, which Jewel clearly was not at the time. Only a relentless work ethic and a love of music got her through the early days of touring.

To help combat that uprooted feeling of being on the road, Jewel carried along a plastic container filled with earth dug from her Alaskan homestead, an eagle's feather, plus pictures of the mountains in Alaska and of her beloved horse Clearwater.

(Jewel loves animals, especially horses. There is an adorable photo at the Atlantic Records Web site of Jewel as a youngster standing next to a horse named Enchantress. But she has said that her all-time favorite was Clearwater. He was sick and in danger of dying when she first got him, but Jewel pampered and nursed him back to health, and he went on to live a full life. She currently has a horse named Jazz whom she loves dearly and takes out riding at every opportunity.)

Zipping from town to town in a given region, Jewel would do weekly residencies in key cities. A "residential tour" is one in which a performer sets up in a hub city then plays at various places in the region, rotating roughly once a week. It's a cost-efficient means for a record company to saturate an area with a particular act. It works best with self-contained solo musicians such as Jewel was at the time.

Her temporary performance homes during this period included Hotel Utah in San Francisco; the Last Drop in Philadelphia; the Escape Cafe in Washington D.C.; Kendall Cafe in Cambridge; Ludlow Cafe in New York City; C'Est What in Toronto, Canada; Urbus Orbus in Chicago; Insomnia in Columbus; Brazil in Detroit; and Puss Puss Cafe in Seattle.

These month-long stints at coffee shops and other intimate spots mirrored her earlier experience at the Innerchange. Most of these solo shows were for little or no cover. Opening night was never easy, with small crowds that were generally not familiar with Jewel or her music. But, as always, her talent brought people back, and word of mouth drew new listeners. By the third or fourth week of each residency, it was often standing room only.

In retrospect, Jewel couldn't help but lament some of the less-appealing gigs. She told a *Detroit Free Press* writer, "I would play in a coffee shop that had a stage that was 3-by-3, like a little postage stamp. . . . I couldn't close my eyes. Everybody talked, and you couldn't make people listen by screaming." Still, she has asserted from the beginning that "a day of long interviews and bad shows is better than one hour of waitressing."

In conjunction with her nightly residential stops, Jewel would play at high schools during the day. One time in Detroit she was booked to do a morning show in the inner city where the school officials got her name confused with that of a rap artist named Jewell.

She also did print, radio, and local TV interviews on an almost daily basis. During this period she frequently involved interviewers in a game she loved to play know as "Would you rather . . . ?" It's a creative word exercise that can lead to surprising personal insights; Jewel has always been very curious about what's going on in other people's minds.

All you have to do to play is make up comparisons and pose them as questions. For example, "Would you rather be a Wiffle ball or a pool ball?" (Jewel prefers the pool ball—but not the eight ball.)

The classic question came to be "Would you rather be a fish or a star?" Jewel's answer, a star, prompted the creators of a fan Web site to arrange for a star to be named after Jewel in honor of her twenty-third birthday. The star, named simply Jewel Kilcher, is positioned in the Little Dipper constellation.

Jewel also loves to watch people, which is one of the reasons she spends so much time in coffee shops. She creates stories in her mind about what the strangers do for a living, where they come from, who they love. . . . As she says, "I make up their lives to be tragic or boring or brilliant or normal."

When touring Jewel uses her vivid and active imagination to engage with the many strangers she meets, and to fight boredom and stress. In childhood it came in handy when times were tough. She recalls, "I used to play a game where I'd pretend I was an eagle. I'd fly up and look down at my life and see how silly it was, how everything would pass."

Pieces of You didn't exactly zoom up the charts when first released, but over a span of months the combination of residencies and interviews proved to be very effective. It wasn't long before Jewel was selling upward of one thousand CDs a week, without much help from the radio programmers and with virtually no exposure on TV.

There seem to be certain acts that, no matter how much they rock the house, aren't able to translate that immediate response into sales. But folks who enjoyed Jewel in a live setting invariably sought out and purchased *Pieces of You*. In cities such as Columbus and Detroit, Jewel's popularity caught fire.

Jewel welcomed the challenge, trusting that her persistence would pay off in the long haul. "I know that hardwood grows slowly, and if I wanted to have a long-term career like Neil Young, it would just take touring," she explained.

Some musicians are primarily studio artists, but Jewel is first and foremost a live performer, so her connection to the fans is direct and interactive. In addition, she is such a prolific songwriter that it becomes difficult even for her to keep track of all her compositions. Fortunately she has a loyal following of home tapers who make nonprofit bootlegs.

The term "bootleg" can have different meanings and implications, depending on whether you're a fan or you work for a record company. For fans, bootlegging represents the only means of obtaining not-officially-released work. For the record companies, it means a perceived loss of revenue.

The collector who smuggles personal recording equipment into a concert venue to capture the event for personal and barter use would subscribe to the following definition of bootlegs: illicitly made recordings that are sold *for profit* in violation of copyright. In other words, true bootlegging is a crime that gives concert taping a bad name.

However, as self-appointed documenters of music history, amateur tapers provide a service that is invaluable to the fans who crave more material than the record conglomerates care to put out. They help promote the artist and increase the fan base, in addition to keeping the interest of hardcore followers fresh.

This is especially relevant in Jewel's case. The lengthy gap between her first official release and her second has been beneficial for Atlantic, who justifiably milked *Pieces of You* for all it was worth. But the fans who've been into Jewel since 1995 or before would have been starving for new Jewel material had it not been for the concert tapers.

The quintessential taper's band was the Grateful Dead, who went so far as to provide a specific seating section for personal recording at their shows. Recent artists who have carried on that ethic include the Dave Matthews Band, Widespread Panic, and Metallica.

An example of a Jewel set list from her residency period might have included such unreleased tidbits as: "I Got the Blues More than You Do Blues," "All the Animals," "Dance Between Two Women," "The Man Who's Already Gone," and literally dozens of other great songs (in all their various versions) that the home tapers preserved.

Many of Jewel's musical highlights might have been lost to the moment had someone in the crowd not seen fit to record them. Her bond with the fans can only be stronger for permitting such nonprofit taping to continue. "If it wasn't for my fans sending me back the bootlegs the stuff would be gone forever," Jewel once said in an interview with *Spinonline.*

When she wasn't going it alone in a high school or coffeehouse, Jewel was the opener for an eclectic variety of artists. The people at Atlantic trusted that Jewel could impress even the toughest audiences, and that's exactly what she frequently faced. Some of the acts with whom Jewel shared live billing included:

Jeff Buckley

With his 1994 debut, *Grace,* Jeff Buckley (son of underground legend Tim Buckley) scored a major critical success. A gifted writer, guitarist, and vocalist, he melted down jazz, blues, and rock to forge well-crafted pop songs. Jewel opened for Buckley at San Diego's Hahn Cosmopolitan Theater just prior to recording *Pieces of You* at the Innerchange. (Buckley drowned in Memphis in 1997.)

Peter Murphy

Murphy's band Bauhaus was the seminal creepy art-pop group of the '80s, and he's been called the "godfather of Gothic Rock." He was the first of the Atlantic artists who agreed to accept Jewel as an opener, but his hyper-produced aesthetic makes for the most un-Jewel-like music imaginable. Jewel opened for Murphy several times in the summer of 1995 and wasn't always politely received by his fans.

Deep Blue Something

These one-hit wonders were responsible for the infectious hit "Breakfast at Tiffany's." Jewel opened for them about a half dozen times on the East Coast in early October 1995, and she played solo at a Washington, D.C., concert at which Deep Blue Something cancelled.

Catherine Wheel / Belly

British rockers whose swirling, guitar-based songs are a cat's cradle of emotion and sonic release, Catherine Wheel is one of the more underrated UK bands in America, but they have little in common, musically, with Jewel.

Tanya Donnelly, who teamed with Kristin Hersch in Throwing Muses and Kim Deal in the Breeders, was the force behind Belly. They had a couple of minor hits on alternative radio before breaking up in 1996.

Jewel was the warm-up act for Catherine Wheel and Belly for roughly eight East Coast and Midwest shows in October 1995. She had to skip a couple of her scheduled appearances due to illness.

John Hiatt

A country-folk-pop songsmith, Hiatt isn't a hit machine, but his CD masterpiece *Bring the Family* was one of the best releases of the past twenty-five years. Jewel has cited him as one of her favorite songwriters, and she covered his "Have a Little Faith in Me" for the *Phenomenon* soundtrack. She played a series of New England dates with him in December 1995.

Liz Phair

Phair's debut CD, *Exile in Guyville,* was an indie success story in 1993–94. Asked how it felt to open for Liz Phair, Jewel said, "I was so scared, you know, I worship her." It's an especially interesting comment in light of Phair's own well-publicized bouts of stage fright.

Dave Matthews Band

South African expatriate Dave Matthews fronts one of the tightest rock bands you'll ever see. Prime movers in the post–Grateful Dead era, the DMB have encouraged home taping (as has Jewel) among their grassroots followers, going so far as to provide a soundboard patch-in until profiteering bootleggers spoiled the fun. Jewel was DMB's opener at Boston's Orpheum in December 1995.

While she shared at least a parcel of common musical ground with most of the acts for which she opened—Peter Murphy being an extreme exception—appearing with such a cornucopia of acts had its ups and downs.

On the positive side, Jewel was able to reach listeners who wouldn't otherwise have heard her music, and it gave her a chance to sharpen her performance skills in front of neutral audiences. She had to win them over, which meant bringing all her energy to every concert.

The situation also put her creativity into overdrive by exposing her to bands she might not have otherwise seen. For a musician, every exposure to other bands is useful; if they rock, it can be motivational. Whether their style is edgy, cool, whatever—there's always at least some small element you can cop for yourself.

On the negative side, it isn't easy playing for another performer's fans, especially when they are anxiously anticipating the headliner. Jewel didn't have the luxury of being pumped up by an adoring crowd; she needed to burn from the first note and create momentum on her own.

Most nights she did just that. The few times she

came out flat were understandable, especially considering that she was living on a nightly average of three or four hours sleep and driving herself to and from gigs; no tour buses or entourage for a lone young woman with an acoustic guitar.

"You really have to stay very focused and dedicated to what you're doing and always stay joyful and thankful," Jewel says. "Otherwise it's very easy to become over exhausted and begin taking things for granted."

Rough as road life occasionally became, Jewel rarely let anything stop her. The days of singing with her father all over Alaska prepared her for tough crowds. Jewel recalls being in a veterans bar once, where "our audience was, like, three guys with missing limbs wasted out of their minds. I was in a bad mood from arguing with my dad. . . . Then this drunk told me, 'Stop looking so goddamned depressed.' So now when I get onstage, no matter what mood I'm in, I do a good show."

That's life on the road; some shows are better than others. But of all the acts with whom Jewel shared a marquee in the early days of her career, none were more memorable and special than Neil Young and Bob Dylan, two artists whom Jewel admires as much for their integrity and dedication as for their musical gifts.

Neil Young

One of the most influential of modern American songwriters, Neil Young created such classic albums as *Everybody Knows This Is Nowhere*, *On the Beach*, *Rust Never Sleeps*, and *Harvest*. He's been a huge influence on recent generations of musicians, from roots-rock to grunge, and is arguably the coolest musician on the planet.

Neil has been called the "Godfather of Grunge," the forebear of the sound of sonically gritty bands like Nirvana and Pearl Jam; his guitar solo in the song "Cinnamon Girl" could be called the first stroke of what would later become the Pacific Northwest texture. He plays his instrument with gut-twisting emotion and has written some of the most honest lyrics in rock history.

His quieter, primarily acoustic work, for example "The Needle and the Damage Done," has also touched modern pop-folk musicians such as Jewel. In fact, she has said that the words to "Little Sister" were partly inspired by that very song. A close listen reveals that the opening notes of "You Were Meant for Me" also seem to have been influenced by the guitar line in "The Needle and the Damage Done."

Of course, there is also the more direct connection between Neil and Jewel. Not only did the producer of *Pieces of You*, Ben Keith, work with Neil on *Harvest*, the studio work on *Pieces of You* was done at Neil's ranch.

Jewel was the opening act for three weeks' worth of Neil's concerts during August 1996. "Working with Neil was awesome. He's such a sweet man," she enthused. Jewel also has been known to belt out a beautiful cover of Neil's "Love Is a Rose" as an encore to her concerts, complete with yodeling.

Bob Dylan

One of the biggest moments of Jewel's career came when she was picked to open for Bob Dylan on the second night of a five-show run at the historic El Rey Theater in Los Angeles.

She played a forty-five-minute set featuring songs from *Pieces of You*, plus "Deep Water," "Enter from the East," and "Last Dance Rodeo." Then she was called out to sing "I Shall Be Released," sharing a mic with the man himself. Ex-Beatles drummer (and former Shining Time Station narrator) Ringo Starr was among the 865 fans in attendance.

Bob Dylan has arguably been American music's most influential lyricist. At the first-ever Rock-and-Roll Hall of Fame induction dinner, Bruce Springsteen said, "Bob freed your mind the way Elvis freed your body. He had the vision and the talent to make a pop record that contained the whole world."

Jewel also opened for Dylan on a series of five East Coast dates in April 1996. Meeting an icon, much less practicing your art in his presence, can be a very intimidating experience, especially for someone who had yet to reach her twenty-third birthday. Jewel told a reporter from the *Boston Globe*, "He asked me later to recite some of the lyrics of my songs, but I was too embarrassed."

Time will tell if Jewel grows to fulfill the vast promise shown at this early period of her career, but there's no question that she is doing her part to carry on the Dylan legacy. Like the legend, Jewel's thoughtfully poetic lyrics often call for social change but also speak of difficult loves and crises of the soul.

The feel of Jewel's work might be more upbeat and optimistic than Dylan's, but that doesn't imply that he is any less inspirational or that she is any less pragmatic. They may enter through different doors and live on separate floors, but they are certainly neighbors in the Tower of Song.

Jewel put it this way: "The coolest thing ever? Singing with Bob Dylan . . . I was blown away. . . . And just talking to him is hilarious, you know?" Jewel even tweaked Dylan's nose, a claim few other musicians can make. "I got to sing with Bob Dylan, I got to smell his garlic breath," Jewel giddily reported.

Jewel was even touted as "the next Bob Dylan" by a certain famous movie actor, which for better or worse brings up another subject, one that invariably has gotten an icy response from Jewel.

As unreal as it may have seemed to Jewel, she was en route to being famous. Unfortunately recognition exacts a price, and it isn't always a fair one. Parts of life that should be private can get dragged into the public forum. Fans want to know everything about their favorite stars, and the media sometimes will do anything to feed that desire.

The more personal and intimate the gossip, the more careful the reporters should be to get the story right or not talk about it at all. Sadly, that priority can get turned upside down. The celebrity tries to keep his or her personal life secret, so the gossip mongers dig up half the truth or a rumor and put it in print.

That being understood, it's best to stick to facts when discussing Jewel's relationship with Sean Penn. And frankly, there isn't that much to tell. Sean saw Jewel perform on the Conan O'Brien show and was, not surprisingly, knocked out by her talent. He championed her to the press and suggested that she could be the next Bob Dylan, which is essentially the highest praise that could be given to a young songwriter.

Jewel and Sean eventually met and spent time together at the Venice Film Festival, where talk of a romantic link began to percolate. The press stirred up interest from fans of both Sean and Jewel, and before long the gossip was too hot to cool down. Oddly enough, Sean had taken to living in an Airstream trailer on his property in Los Angeles during the time he was seeing Jewel, who had not so long ago been living in a van herself.

Jewel tended to bristle when the subject came up, usually expressing the sentiment that it was nobody's business and that she felt as if the tabloid papers were writing about a fictional character, someone other than her.

The pair later teamed up artistically on a couple of projects. Jewel wrote a song called "Emily" for a film, *The Crossing Guard*, that Sean wrote and directed. Sean directed a video for Jewel's "You Were Meant for Me" that included a scene of Jewel watching a fictional boyfriend kissing an unknown woman. Jewel eventually decided that the video "didn't fit the song," and it was reshot with a different director.

In early 1996 Sean married the mother of his two children, actress Robin Wright, and that was essentially the end of the story, although it was hardly the last time that Jewel was asked about it. Jewel later told *Details* magazine, "It was what it was, but compared to the duration of other relationships I've had, it was so not a big deal."

The disheartening Sean Penn media frenzy hasn't been the only instance in which the press gave

Jewel a hard time. Like anyone who isn't afraid to take risks in public, she has felt the sting of criticism. She has even written at least two brief but intense poems on the subject, one of which appears on the inner sleeve of *Pieces of You*.

The same openness that makes Jewel's work so inspirational to her fans also exposes her to criticism by the often cynical music press. It's precisely the type of issue she addresses in "I'm Sensitive."

An early review of *Pieces of You*, in a 1995 edition of the *Washington Post*, praised Jewel's voice but referred to "an unfortunate tendency to present trite, hackneyed sentiments as if they were oracular visions from a young prophet to a jaded world."

Perhaps not everyone is inspired by Jewel-isms such as "hands manifest thought," or "in silence you create yourself," but for those who haven't come across these ideas, Jewel is as worthy a source as any. It hardly makes the world a worse place for such concepts to be given voice, no matter how often or by whom.

Some attacks were so spiteful that they seemed to reveal more about the reviewer's state of mind than about Jewel's music. In one instance, between songs during a 1997 concert at New York City's Beacon Theater, she told the crowd that "I don't really think any one of us is truly alone," and "I think by nature we're good."

One local critic referred to her words as "sugary pronouncements" in a review that was snidely titled "Jewel Cops a Platitude." The writer took a swipe at both Jewel and her fans, implying that her popularity is dependent on "young audiences seeking guidance."

Jewel's philosophy on such attitudes is reflected in comments she made to Jon Stewart: "Cynicism isn't smarter, it's only safer. There's nothing fluffy about optimism. It's just a matter of people being more fulfilled and more whole as human beings."

What is it that Jewel's critics don't grasp that comes through so clearly to her fans? Why do they react so harshly to Jewel and her songs? Her take on the phenomenon is this: "I think some of them are working out their lives on paper. They're bummed about their life and [the music] reminds them of something."

And she's absolutely right. It's all about the difference between beauty and the sublime: beauty doesn't need to be processed through the intellect, it can be taken in unfiltered. Critics are all about analyzing that which is beyond analysis. Jewel put it this way on the 1997 Grammy Awards preview show: "Music touches people's hearts . . . it doesn't go through your mental capacity."

Sometimes the most reactionary critics are formerly the biggest idealists of all, but the hard knocks of life have made them prone to snapping and snarling at anything that reminds them of their own sensitivity. A lot of people don't trust beauty when they encounter it, and some folks even respond by attacking. Maybe the critics who attack Jewel do so because she's pieces of them.

Whatever the reason, they'll always offer explanations for why we shouldn't enjoy what we do enjoy. Trust that Jewel will keep doing what her heart tells her, whether the press likes it or not. As she says, "the fans get it," and that's what counts.

CHAPTER NINE

❧

Catching the Wave

Jewel recalls that her first surfing experience—
that is, her first wave—was exactly what she
thought it would be and yet more awesome than
she could have imagined. She felt very much at
risk, but she loved the rush. It was the same with
the first waves of fame that came crashing in to
her life.

One evening, not very long after the release of
Pieces of You, Jewel was driving from Los Angeles
back to San Diego. She was tuned in to a local radio program that counts down the station's top
nine most-requested songs.

As she rode along with a friend, listening to the
likes of Pearl Jam and Nirvana, Jewel couldn't help
thinking that she'd never write songs that were good
enough to compete with what she was hearing.

You know what's coming. When the DJ an-
nounced the number-one song, it was Jewel's own

"Who Will Save Your Soul." Taken by surprise and deliriously excited, Jewel began pounding her driving companion's leg, shrieking, "Oh my God, that's me! That's me!"

By the spring of 1996 she was in the midst of a headlining tour—the Tour of Tiny Lights. The Rugburns, with John Castro on bass and John Aafedt on drums, were her opening act for several dates, and they frequently joined her onstage. Jewel and Steve Poltz would sing "You Were Meant for Me" together. At other times, she was accompanied by a virtuoso cellist named John Fagen, who played beautifully on songs such as "Enter from the East."

In keeping with the tour's name, there were dozens of simulated candles surrounding Jewel onstage. She had worked on the lighting herself, saying she felt it made for "a certain mystical experience." Behind her were huge screens that flashed images to match the songs: a cowboy for the yodeling song "Chime Bells," church rafters for "Angel Standing By" and "Amen," and so on.

Summing up just how far Jewel had come, a reviewer for *Hollywood Reporter* wrote of Jewel's show at the Wiltern Theater, "Two years ago, when Atlantic first released Jewel's *Pieces of You*, the singer-songwriter opened for Liz Phair at this venue. Same album, two years later, the singer/songwriter is headlining two sold-out nights."

Even after she'd been touring for more than a year in support of her CD, playing to all sizes and stripes of audience, Jewel was still overwhelmed by the crowds that gathered to see and hear her.

"There's a lot of you . . . and only one of me!" she told fans at Mann Music Center in Philadelphia before playing a forty-minute set as part of a music festival. Whereas she had been playing for fewer than fifty people in coffee shops and clubs, Jewel was now drawing thousands.

The attention had come "first gradually, then suddenly," as the old saying goes, and it took some getting used to. Jewel reflected, "As a girl I used to go out to the meadows and pray. And now I go in the bathrooms to check in: 'How you doing, Jewel?' "

She played a sold-out show at Berkeley Community Theater—a four-thousand-seat venue—and received three standing ovations. Jewel humbly and graciously thanked the fans, with a depth of feeling that matched what they were offering her. It was exactly the kind of reciprocal exchange that she has often said gives her the most pleasure in playing live—that bridging of the space between audience and artist, person and person.

"I think it's sad that so many people do feel separate from each other and that's why I sing," she explained in a Toronto television interview. "It's 'cause you feel very connected to people and, at least in that moment, people feel kind of together."

Such situations were becoming the norm, and Jewel's popularity was increasing exponentially with the long-delayed help of radio and video stations, who had finally caught on to the mass appeal of what she was offering. Still, she never lost sight of who really deserved the credit for her growing success: the fans.

At the third annual BFD festival, a benefit for Tibet that was held at the San Francisco Bay Area's Shoreline Amphitheater, she told her audience, "I can't believe I'm in front of all you people. . . . It's because you guys buy my album and the radio plays it that I get to eat. So, thank you for coming."

She wasn't paying lip service to get the crowd on her side—she was well aware of the difference between where she'd been and where she was. Jewel told a reporter for *Access Hollywood*, "I have a new car, I don't worry about eating, I don't worry about getting sick and being able to afford a doctor . . . the biggest thing to me is I do feel like I have a purpose. And I think everybody wants that, and I feel I'm so glad to have it."

In 1996 Jewel won the Favorite New Artist award at the American Music Awards. A few months later, the Alaska House and Senate issued a citation congratulating their "favorite daughter." The citation read in part: "Her unique style, from folk to a jazzy new age, her powerful haunting delivery, and her soul-baring lyrics have earned her favorable reviews from coast to coast."

High praise. Beyond praise, actually. Almost glorification when taken in concert with all the acclaim from fans, critics, and the like. Imagine having the back of your hand kissed by the house and senate of the state where you grew up. It takes inner strength to keep that sort of thing from sweeping you off to never-never land. It's like riding a tsunami.

Jewel is well aware that she must keep it all in perspective. As she has frequently noted, it's tempting to take flattery as a true reflection of self. "If you believe that," she warns, "you become relative to it. Then you're only as good as your last compliment or critique."

Jewel's first headlining tour was a wild success, as she held one sold-out audience after another in the palm of her hand. She was joined on the road in June 1996 by another young Atlantic artist, Duncan Sheik, whose self-titled debut had just been released and who would go on to have a smash hit with "Barely Breathing." Jewel and Duncan often sang his song "Home" onstage together.

Jewel had come such a long way. What artist wouldn't prefer having her own fans—for instance the young women who held up signs proclaiming that they were "maintaining their innocence"—at her own shows? *Pieces of You* had just turned Gold (500,000 sold), and Jewel's career was reaching a comfort zone.

CHAPTER TEN

Attack of the TV Babies

Clearly, constant touring was the foundation of Jewel's increasing popularity, but millions of music fans nevertheless first laid eyes on her in music videos and television specials such as VH1's *Duets*, where she sang "Foolish Games" and "You Can Sleep While I Drive" with Melissa Etheridge.

These days, big sales in the music biz are generated as much by the channel changer as by the radio dial. Being part of the regular rotation on video networks is both a stamp of arrival and a ticket to the next level for the vast majority of modern musicians.

There's no question that Jewel would have eventually made it without television; her talent and energy were enough to make her a star no matter what. But showing up on MTV and VH1 several times a day made it a lot quicker and easier.

It was poetic justice that Jewel became a video

staple after the powers that be had previously deemed her music unsellable. It simply became clear that she was too good to be ignored. Jewel's beauty and charisma were natural visual accompaniments to her dramatic songs.

By the end of March 1996, MTV was playing "Who Will Save Your Soul" several times each day, and at the 1996 MTV Video Music Awards, she scored two nominations on the strength of "Who Will Save Your Soul." One was for Best Female Video, the other was for Best New Artist. She lost both categories to Alanis Morissette, but that didn't diminish Jewel's momentum.

A new video had been shot in August to replace Sean Penn's interpretation of "You Were Meant for Me." It was released the day after the MTV Awards show aired, and it was quick to crack the network's rotation. Jewel was also showing up on various MTV shows, such as *Alternative Nation* and *120 Minutes*.

Riding the wave of popularity spawned by her videos, Jewel would eventually check in with an appearance on MTV's *Unplugged* series, which feature's primarily rock artists in an acoustic setting. In an acoustic context the songs must stand on their own, and the artist with them.

Taking away the volume and distortion separates the grown-ups from the children, so to speak. In this regard, Jewel had been a mature artist for quite a while. In June 1997, Jewel made her appearance on *Unplugged*, playing at the beautiful Brooklyn Academy of Music, with musical direction by Don Was. The show had been taped in May and aired a month and a half later.

Along with the four singles from *Pieces of You*, she belted out keeper versions of "Boy Needs a Bike," "Satellite," "Last Dance Rodeo," "Fragile Flame," "Passing Time," and the Cole Porter treasure "Too Darn Hot" (from the musical *Kiss Me Kate*). It was a satisfying mix to say the least, delivered with Jewel's trademark verve. As a special treat—one that new fans may have found surprising—Jewel plugged in to become fully amplified and band-backed on a few numbers.

Less than three months after she was on *Unplugged*, "You Were Meant for Me" was nominated for a trio of 1997 MTV Video Music Awards. Jewel performed at the show, but she elected not to play any of the songs from *Pieces of You*, opting instead for old favorite "Angel Standing By," presumably in honor of Mother Teresa and Princess Diana, both of whom had died just days earlier. The categories and the nominees were as follows:

Best Video of the Year

"The New Pollution" by Beck
"Virtual Insanity" by Jamiroquai

"You Were Meant for Me" by Jewel
"The Perfect Drug" by Nine Inch Nails
"Don't Speak" by No Doubt

Best Female Video

"On and On" by Erykah Badu
"Un-Break My Heart" by Toni Braxton
"Bitch" by Meredith Brooks
"Where Have All the Cowboys Gone" by Paula
    Cole
"You Were Meant for Me" by Jewel

Viewers Choice

"You Were Meant for Me" by Jewel
"Breathe" by Prodigy
"I'll Be Missing You" by Puff Daddy, featuring Faith
    Evans & 122
"Say You'll Be There" by the Spice Girls
"One Headlight" by the Wallflowers

Jewel was the only artist to be selected for
consideration in all three categories, and she took
home the award for Best Female Video. She lost
Best Video of the Year to Jamiroquai and Viewers
Choice to Prodigy.

By the time the *Unplugged* tape finally hit the

small screen in mid-July, "Foolish Games" was already in stress rotation on MTV.

VH1, the MTV-owned network whose format is geared more toward the so-called adult contemporary market, also played a huge part in Jewel's arrival. Her appearance on *Duets* with Melissa Etheridge in October 1995 created a strong buzz, as Jewel's versatility and universal appeal were fully on display.

So important was VH1's role that when the nation's largest cable operator took it off the air in Denver, Jewel was one of a group of musicians, including Don Henley and John Mellencamp, who protested the move and lobbied for VH1's reinstatment.

As further proof of Jewel's status, the "You Were Meant for Me" video was given the treatment on an episode of VH1's *Pop-Up Video*. For those who are unfamiliar with the show, it features music videos embellished with information bubbles that deliver quirky facts related (sometimes very loosely) to the videos and the artists: for example, the dry comment "Well-proportioned jewels are the most valuable," as a double entendre in reference to Jewel's figure.

Jewel also kicked off the VH1 network's *Hard Rock Live* series, playing a ten-song set and being joined onstage by her parents for yodeling and a cappella singing. A glimpse backstage, including a

brief conversation with fellow Lilith Fair partici-
pant Paula Cole, added to a great hour of Jewel at
her best.

Of course, VH1 also ran Jewel's videos several
times each day, and when the network counted
down the top fifty videos of 1997, "You Were
Meant for Me" came in at number eleven, while
"Foolish Games" was number two.

Jewel's non–MTV/VH1 television appearances
and interviews (of which there are too many to
list) have included: Regis & Kathie Lee, Conan
O'Brien, David Letterman, Lauren Hutton, *The
Tonight Show*, *Good Morning America*, *CBS This
Morning*, Rosie O'Donnell, Charlie Rose, and Tom
Snyder. Jewel also made encore appearances on
most of these shows.

She was on *Saturday Night Live* in May 1997, at
one point playing herself for a skit in which she
was snowbound with comedian Jon Lovitz in a log
cabin, repeating the same stories over and over.
The show was reaired a couple of months later. It
was fitting that Jewel, who'd grown up without
television and been ignored by the networks at
the start of her career, had now conquered the
medium so completely.

The situation was similar with regard to radio.
In general the programmers had been downright
snippy in response to suggestions that Jewel's music was worthy of airplay. It's a fairly typical sce-

nario, but that's one of the bad things that happen when art and money get mixed together.

It's complicated. The musicians tend to see it as Doc Driscoll, formerly of the Rugburns, does; to wit: "Remind me to tell you someday how much I hate radio. It's all a big sham, fooling people into thinking they're listening to stuff they like when actually their taste is manipulated by corporations that do market research, as though music were a commodity like toilet paper."

There are quite a few bands that should be so useful as toilet paper, but that's beside the point. As pleasurable as it would be to take a sledgehammer to the ivory towers, it's as much the fans and the bands who are to blame as it is the suits for the current state of affairs. If the masses are being fooled—and it takes some condescension to reach that conclusion—they've no one to blame but themselves, and if the bands are in it for fame and fortune, then they shouldn't whine when their art goes in the same bin as hot dogs, toilet paper, etc.

The record companies tend to be more reactionary than manipulative in their methods. They sift through the available talent, sign the acts that sound like something people are already buying, then take their chances. Most of the time the closest a music publisher comes to market research is polling the people in the adjoining offices about what their teenagers are listening to that week.

Jewel's case is a perfect example. The better part

of two years passed before her career took off like a rocket. In the interim it was more like a slow boat. As Ron Shapiro pithily put it, "No one wanted to know from her initially." As it turned out, she wound up being positioned alongside Celine Dion and Chumbawamba on radio playlists, which indicates either free-market randomness or the most cleverly disguised conspiracy in music history.

All this isn't to say that music corporations can't be creepy and that radio programmers don't severely underestimate listener intelligence. But sometimes things work out anyway. Atlantic stuck with Jewel because key people in the company believed in her, and radio caught on when the financial benefits grew too obvious to ignore, which is about all that's reasonable to expect in a society where cash is king.

Of course, it was still a pleasure for Jewel to go from persona non grata to V.I.P. on the airwaves. "It's fun to see all the people kiss my butt that said they would play my records on the radio over their dead bodies," she proclaimed in *New Musical Express*.

CHAPTER ELEVEN

Playing Politics

> "Why are so many adults in suits doing the
> Macarena at the Democratic convention?"
> —Jewel

While at the time she didn't consider herself particularly politically minded, asserting, "I'm too young to be, but I'm learning," Jewel attended the 1996 Democratic National Convention. She even did some reporting for MTV, posing questions to officials and delegates on the convention floor.

For example, she asked Robert Reich, Secretary of the U.S. Department of Labor, what values his party wanted to show the youth of America. His reply: "tolerance, inclusion of all people," seemed to sum up the general theme of the event and echo Jewel's philosophy as well.

When being questioned herself during an MTV online chat at the convention, Jewel cut through much of the rhetoric by saying, "Both parties are talking about children being the hope of the future, but I want to know, who is the hope of today?" Either instinctively or by design, Jewel tends to present her ideas as questions, encouraging people to find the answers for themselves.

After Bill Clinton was reelected for a second term, Jewel was invited to be one of the performers at his inauguration party in January 1997. Jewel initially turned down the prestigious opportunity, but then she received a very special phone call—from President Clinton himself! "We missed the call of all things," she said, "but I heard this message and said 'Oh my God!' " Of course, Jewel then agreed to attend.

There were fifteen different inaugural balls featuring such luminary musicians as fiddler Bela Fleck, pianist Bruce Hornsby, former Grateful Dead guitarist Bob Weir, and Joni Mitchell.

All the balls were briefly attended by the Clinton family. Jewel played at an event called the 21st Century Ball and shared stage time with LL Cool J and others. "I'm glad to see that all of America isn't cynical," Jewel was heard to comment.

A year later Jewel joined with a disparate variety of musicians—Anita Baker, Michael Bolton, and Mary-Chapin Carpenter, among others—in Washington, D.C., to encourage the U.S. Congress to support the arts in education. The National Academy of the Recording Arts and Sciences sponsored the event, and the musicians visited area schools to spread their message.

Rock and politics are the strangest of bedfellows. The powers that be try to absorb and use for their own purposes that which is inherently antiestablishment, i.e., rock 'n' roll, while many artists can't resist the temptation to try to change the world.

But there is a middle realm between being overtly political and speaking to the human concerns that politics were spawned to address. "I never considered myself to be particularly politically oriented," Jewel has said. "However, we are all humans, we all live here, so it has just been a natural humanitarian interest."

In mid-December 1997, Jewel joined Mariah Carey, Sinead O'Connor, and other artists in Oslo, Norway, for a benefit concert to honor antilandmine activist Jody Williams, who had been awarded the Nobel Peace Prize. One of Jewel's musical heroines, Joan Osborne, had performed at the previous year's Nobel concert, the first time that the program featured music other than classical.

Although she might be linked in some people's minds to the so-called '60s resurgence because of what's perceived as her folk-music roots, Jewel gently scoffs at the notion that she is some kind of hippie. As she told Joe Deltufo of *Big Shout*, "It's not us against them anymore. It's just us. . . ."

CHAPTER TWELVE

∞

Crowning Jewel's Achievements

Constant touring, mixed with increased media exposure, had expanded Jewel's fan base and burned her name into the musical landscape. "When I sold 8,000 records in one week, I remember crying on my kitchen floor, thanking God that I might never have to waitress or live in my car again," Jewel told *Rolling Stone*.

That was only the beginning. In the final week of April 1996 *Pieces of You* had sold 22,000 copies. In the same week exactly one year before—two months following its release—it had sold fewer than 700 units nationwide. After cracking the *Billboard* album chart in early 1996, *Pieces of You* made a steady ascent on the wings of "Who Will Save Your Soul" and nonstop touring.

Keep in mind, Jewel never thought she'd get a recording contract. When she did, she thought her CD might sell 40,000 copies total. It took a full fourteen months of sweat and perseverance, but she had managed to fulfill half her original expectation in the span of only seven days!

For a person whose personal philosophy is faith-based, with belief in herself (plus the occasional assistance of angels) at the core, it doesn't seem to jibe that Jewel would have underestimated her success so severely. Perhaps the reason for the apparent contradiction is that Jewel is a worrier at heart. She knows that things will turn out okay, but she frets until they actually do. Then she worries about whatever comes next. "I only ever wanted to do things that made me feel at rest because I've always felt so driven and pushed," she said.

Of course, uncertainty can be a strong motivational force, and Jewel obviously uses nervous energy to her advantage, which is probably part of the reason why situations tend to come out well for her in the end.

Take, for instance, the Cafe Crema story. In 1993 Jewel auditioned for a chance to play at a San Diego coffeehouse called Cafe Crema. She failed to impress the then-owner and didn't get the gig.

In a classic instance of the spiral-shaped nature of life, Jewel finally got to play for an audience at Cafe Crema—three years after that unsuccessful tryout. Jewel was sitting alone at a table in Cafe Crema, jotting down poetry and drinking coffee.

She was taking a rest from her hectic touring schedule, using the time to catch up on her writing. A local acoustic guitarist was preparing to begin his set. The musician, Rick Fagen, happened to be a regional sales manager for Taylor guitars, which, according to the liner notes in *Pieces of You*, is Jewel's favorite brand.

Fagen noticed that the young woman scribbling away by herself looked very familiar. When he made the connection that it was none other than Jewel, he asked her to play a couple of songs to warm up the crowd, some of whom never realized who his opening act really was. Jewel borrowed Fagen's guitar and happily obliged, making her first performance at Cafe Crema.

So things have a way of coming full circle for Jewel, whether it's playing at Cafe Crema or being accepted by video and radio programmers. Of course, talent has a little something to do with it, and so does experience.

Experience might not be the first word that pops to mind when discussing an artist as young as Jewel, but when you think about it she has probably performed for an audience in some context (radio, TV, concert, etc.) in the neighborhood of six hundred times since she began playing her own music for pay. At this point she's a pro; it's that simple.

And, like everything about her, not so simple.

Does she know how to work a crowd? Does she ever. There's a story attached to just about every one of her hundreds of songs, and she seems to pull out new ones at will. Jewel leads a very adventurous and unsheltered life, immersed in music and touring, which provides anecdotes galore.

Sometimes they're hilarious, like the now-legendary "You Were Meant for Me" story. It wouldn't be rock 'n' roll if drugs didn't crop up from time to time, and even if Jewel doesn't personally indulge, she certainly isn't afraid to approach the subject from various angles. Take, for instance, the line in "Race Car Driver" in which the would-be paramour tells her, "It's better than watching *Star Trek* after you've smoked weed."

At her concerts, Jewel frequently tells about the strange event that happened to her when traveling in Mexico with Steve Poltz. Jewel sprinkles the humorous narrative with a self-mockingly cute voice to represent how naive she was at the time.

It seems that the vacationing couple was looking for a boat to take them whale watching. A group of local police officers offered to take them out, but midway into the trip, Jewel and Steve discovered that the Federales were out on a drug bust. The lawmen even offered the two startled tourists machine guns so they could help nab the dealers. "Here I am in a bikini, saying, 'Are you sure this is proper procedure?' " recalls Jewel. It

turned out to be a successful raid, as the cops net-
ted some five hundred kilos of marijuana stacked
in potato sacks.

The cops insisted that Jewel and Steve take all
the pot they could carry. At this point in the tale,
Jewel points out the irony in the fact that someone
who "doesn't even smoke" would find herself ordered by the authorities to take a stash of marijuana. (She makes an aside joke that maybe Alanis
Morissette should include that in her song "Isn't It
Ironic.") Jewel and Steve obliged, then passed the
haul along to the cook who worked at the rundown
resort where they were staying. "She needed it for
her arthritis," says Jewel with a knowing wink. She
tells the story as an introduction to "You Were
Meant for Me" because the song was written by
Steve and Jewel on that trip.

On the general topic of mind-altering sub-
stances, Jewel is essentially chemical free, even
with regard to alcohol. She got an up-close look at
the perils of that particular drug when she was
touring the bars of Alaska with her father.

She recalls one fellow in particular, who was a
regular at a local bar. It seems the guy would plunk
down his cash and drain a couple of pitchers of
beer in an evening. He'd request the same sad
songs each time, then offer young Jewel her
choice of the bills on his table. "I'd always take a
twenty, and get a Shirley Temple with it. And he'd
get hammered," she remembers. As it turns out,

the poor guy had been a medic in Vietnam. One night the vet went home and shot himself to death. The sad incident made a powerful impression on Jewel, who sums up the story by saying, "I remember thinking that I don't want to hide behind things. I decided right then and there that I never wanted to drink."

As you can see, some of her tales aren't funny at all. In any event, you never know what Jewel is going to say or do onstage, but you know it'll be something engaging. She takes requests and song polls ("cheer if you'd rather hear 'Little Sister' or 'Pieces of You' "), makes wisecracks, and is always ready with a hearty "f*#k you" for the boys who misbehave.

Best of all, she isn't afraid to be herself. Jewel has been known to scribble down one or two brand-new songs before going onstage, then try them out for the crowd with a comment such as, "I don't know how good this is, but at least it's new," or a simple "I've never sung this in front of people before." She'll even read the lyrics out of a notebook if she hasn't had time to memorize them. Jewel flares her nostrils and cries out in discomfort when her guitar isn't in tune, rather than trying to hide the fact. She'll pose with a distorted face, self-mocking the way she looks when she's photographed in the act of singing.

With all due respect to Jagger and Richards, et al., you aren't likely to get that level of spontaneity from, say, a Rolling Stones show. In that sense—perhaps the most important sense—Jewel rocks. But she also has a sense for just how far to push it, and she'll always follow her goofy moments with something so artfully polished that it makes you fall in love with her even more than you already were.

And that could well be the key to Jewel's stage-side manner. The more energy that the audience feeds her, the more Jewel sends back to them. "An audience is like a live animal, and you have to read its body language . . ." she explains.

Few artists are as adept as she is at helping the people in the crowd feel connected to what's happening onstage and to each other. The bond is familiar—in so much as the fans are unconditionally devoted, giving Jewel the freedom to experiment, make her mistakes, and inevitably shine. Two cases in point:

Before a concert overseas, Jewel forgot the lyrics to one of her older songs. She called her mother, who contacted the Everyday Angels, who faxed a copy of the words so that Jewel could perform the song. How many musicians have that level of connection to their fans?

At a show in Canada, Jewel forgot the words to "Painters," and was about to give up playing the song for that evening. Instead, she invited a young man who'd been singing along with her to come onstage and help. He came bearing flowers, followed by six friends who also had bouquets for

Jewel. The first guy held a piece of paper with the words so that Jewel could sing them, and she did just that.

Having such a symbiotic relationship with her fans, Jewel is free to reach out and interact with them anytime she likes, thanks in part to the Internet. Just as video influenced an entire generation of musicians and permanently altered the industry in the '80s, the Internet is having a profound effect on the pop artists of the '90s.

Jewel has professed her appreciation for the Internet, explaining that it "takes out the middle men" between her and her fans. She participated in an MTV online interview from the Art Institute of Chicago in August 1996, during which her fans asked questions directly to her, and she answered directly to them.

Still, she doesn't consider herself to be "computer literate." She has cited a poem by Charles Bukowski called "My First Computer Poem," written when he was in his sixties; Jewel lightheartedly speculates that she may be at least that old before she writes her first computer poem.

Ready or not, her life and music are very much a part of cyberspace. A few of Jewel's concerts have been simulcast on the World Wide Web, including one from San Diego by Mediadome. It can be viewed at the following URL: www.mediadome.com.

The Webcast features a few non–*Pieces of You* selections: "Nicotine Love," "Enter from the East," and "Race Car Driver." The Rugburns join Jewel onstage for "You Were Meant for Me," and there is also a "Chime Bells" yodeling segment.

There was another Jewel cybercast, in May 1996 from Irving Plaza in New York City; it was viewed at least in part by an incredible number of people—upward of 275,000. There are literally hundreds of Web sites honoring Jewel that are maintained by fans.

The rapid growth of the Internet has sparked much debate. Will it further fracture an already divided society? Or might it have an opposite but just as detrimental effect, stunting diversity of thought by giving all of us access to identical information at the same time?

Participants in the online discussion group at the address jewel@smoe.org would no doubt assert that the Internet brings people together, and they'd have evidence to back it up. An off-the-cuff request by a list member resulted in an Internet-sparked musical event, as Jewel agreed to play a private concert at Bearsville Theater near Woodstock, New York.

Devoted fans of all ages and lifestyles, privy to the inside scoop, traveled to the site by bus, train, plane, car, brought together by the love of Jewel and her music. The event was dubbed "Jewel-stock," echoing the historic sixties concert that was held not far from the same upstate New York village. On the evening of July 18, 1996, Jewel sang, played, and read poetry for the hundreds of fans who gathered for the special event.

She intentionally didn't play many of her hits, opting instead to focus on lesser-known songs for the Jewel-savvy audience. After the show, Jewel met and talked with her fans and signed autographs before retiring for the evening. The first night's show was free of charge, but some tickets were sold to the public for a second show on the following night, with the proceeds going to the Bearsville Theater.

The locale was convenient for Jewel because it was in close proximity to the studio where she was recording tracks for her second CD. Little did she suspect that more than a year would go by before those recordings would finally be released.

CHAPTER THIRTEEN

☙

Non-*Pieces* Releases

If you aren't a hard-core Jewel aficionado, you may be wondering about the origins of all of these songs that weren't on *Pieces of You*. Where do they come from and how can you get access to them?

An incredibly prolific songwriter, Jewel is constantly creating new songs. Even in the midst of her hectic schedule while promoting *Pieces of You*, she continued to find time for composing fresh material. Since her first efforts at the tender age of seventeen, Jewel has composed well over a hundred beautiful songs.

The first recorded release of a Jewel song came in 1994, when a radio station in San Diego put together a compilation of local bands called *Saint Doug: 91X Alternative Sampler*. Jewel's contribution was an acoustic version of "Angel Needs a Ride."

There have been numerous other Jewel recordings that you might be able to collect from used record stores, by making contact with other fans at concerts, or via the Internet. Making friends with a college radio disc jockey might be your best chance to score one of these rare selections. Good luck!

Promotional Releases

Save the Linoleum

This Atlantic Records promotional release has a humorous black-and-white cover photo that helps explain the unusual title: a small group of "protesters" carry signs that proclaim Linoleum Liberates, Long Live Linoleum, etc. Jewel is shown squatting next to a child in the center of the crowd. Note the live version of "I'm Sensitive" (with a hilarious intro in which Jewel scolds first an audience member and then herself) and the three non–*Pieces of You* selections, including a demo version of "Race Car Driver." This disc has roughly twenty-four minutes of early Jewel at its very best.

1. "God's Gift to Women"
2. "Intro"
3. "I'm Sensitive" (live)

4. "Who Will Save Your Soul"
5. "Race Car Driver"
6. "Flower"
7. "I'm Sensitive"

Shiva Diva Doo Wop

This is one of a couple of hard-to-find items that have cover art created by Jewel herself. She does unique, playful sketches of strange figures behaving strangely. Finding a copy of this will be a real challenge, but what a treasure you'll have if you do manage to locate one. Only one of the four tracks, "Painters," found its way onto her official debut CD.

1. "1,000 Miles Away"
2. "She Cries"
3. "Painters"
4. "God's Gift to Women"

Phyllis Barnaby Finally Gets a Bra

You'll find another out-of-the-ordinary title and a hilarious cover sketch by Jewel on this Atlantic promotional release. Only one of the four tunes was deemed worthy of inclusion on the original release of *Pieces of You*, but the entire lot found its way onto the 1997 vinyl-only release.

1. "You Were Meant for Me"
2. "Cold Song"
3. "Rocker Girl"
4. "Emily"

If you do happen to locate either *Shiva Diva Doo Wop* or *Phyllis Barnaby Finally Gets a Bra*, and you develop a taste for Jewel's slightly esoteric cover artwork, you'll also want to hunt down the Atlantic promo of "You Were Meant for Me." It features a self-portrait of the artist, complete with little fish in her hair, what appears to be a fork inside her stomach, and a halo of thank-yous encircling her head, along with a message of gratitude to those who have helped Jewel's dreams come true. It is signed "Jewel '96."

Music for Films

"Emily" also turned up in Sean Penn's film *The Crossing Guard*. Like the movie, the song is a heartbreaking look at the ways people try to fill the void caused by the loss of a loved one. Jewel has made contributions to a few other film soundtracks including:

A cover of the classic Donovan tune, "Sunshine Superman," was recorded for *I Shot Andy Warhol*.

It's the best version of this song since Husker Dü tore it apart on *Everything Falls Apart* in 1982.

"Have a Little Faith in Me," a wailing (in the good sense) John Hiatt cover, is on the *Phenomenon* soundtrack.

"Under the Water," an uncharacteristically danceable track (it even has a rap sequence reminiscent of Jewel's days in La Creme) is credited to Jewel and R. Sall for *The Craft*.

An alternate version of "Foolish Games" can be heard on the *Batman & Robin* soundtrack but not in the film itself.

You can hear Jewel's cover of Eric Carmen's "All by Myself" in the movie *Clueless*, but it unfortunately was left off the soundtrack CD.

Compilations

If you missed Jewel's performance of "Foolish Games" on VH1's *Crossroads* program, you can catch it on the compilation CD.

A terrific version of "You Were Meant for Me," with bassist Flea from the Red Hot Chili Peppers, can be found on the compilation disc *Live on Letterman: Music from The Late Show.*

The understated but intense "Quiet Warrior" turns up on a benefit CD for the Surfrider Foundation conservation group. The multiple-artist release is titled *M.O.M.: Music for Our Mother Ocean*. Jewel is also on the sequel, *M.O.M. II*, doing the lighthearted "V-12 Cadillac."

Jewel shows up on a couple of tribute albums (those multiartist, cover-song compilations that have become so popular in recent years). She recorded "You Make Lovin' Fun" for a Fleetwood Mac tribute titled *Rumours Revisited*, which is a remake of their classic LP. She also contributed a cover of "Who'll Stop the Rain" for the Creedence Clearwater Revival tribute.

There will also be a Lilith Fair compilation in the near future, on which Jewel will surely be included.

Import Singles

Some of the best sources for obscure Jewel material are the import singles. These CDs, which are official releases in their countries of origin, will typically contain a well-known song plus a couple of bonus selections. They can be ordered in America but are invariably on the pricey side; shelling out ten clams for two new songs isn't uncommon. The options include:

Pieces of You (Japan)

This pressing of Jewel's full-length debut has all the songs from the U.S. release, plus "Emily." It'll run you in the neighborhood of thirty dollars.

Foolish Games (Australia)

The CD single contains the *Batman & Robin* version of "Foolish Games," plus non–*Pieces of You* entries "Everything Breaks Sometimes" and "Angel Needs a Ride."

You Were Meant for Me (European)

This is a CD single with two bonus tracks, "Cold Song" and "Rocker Girl." The cover photo of Jewel lying on a red cloth gazing at a tiny toy sailboat is identical to the one used on the U.S. CD single of "You Were Meant for Me/Foolish Games."

Jewel and her mother sing a duet on a 1997 Christmas CD put out by the Boys Choir of Harlem.

That release, titled *'Tis the Season*, showcases Jewel and Nedra's swinging version of "Rudolph the Red Nosed Reindeer." Their rendition features delightful doo-wop interaction between mother, daughter, and the Choir.

One other item you might try to find is the cassette single that was passed out to the first two hundred people at each of the dates on Jewel's first headlining tour with Atlantic artist Duncan Sheik in May 1996. There are two versions: one has "Emily" and the other "Race Car Driver." Both have "Who Will Save Your Soul" plus a couple of Duncan Sheik songs. The cover shot of Jewel's face in close-up is stunning.

CHAPTER FOURTEEN

She's Got Skills

It's a tricky proposition to analyze the power of music, because it reaches us in ways that are beyond words. Still, it seems worthwhile to discuss what specific qualities made Jewel the new goddess of popular music and *Pieces of You* the brilliant, eight-million seller it is.

Jewel brings the following qualities to all of her work: poetic depth, inspired songwriting, the voice of an angel, artistic integrity and complexity of character, beauty, and spirituality. All that—and she yodels, too!

Writing great lyrics is a matter of using everyday details to evoke the deeper truths that we all feel but can't put into words. This is something that Jewel does with often haunting results. For example, the around-the-house objects in "Morning Song" lift your spirits with memories of happy times, while similar objects in "You Were Meant for Me" can break your heart like an egg. In the cathartic "Amen," Jewel mixes mystical imagery with scary details of a life in mortal pain.

She has mastered the songwriter's craft of elevating the listener's soul with music while, at the same time, keeping it grounded in reality with thoughtful, pragmatic words. She sinks her teeth into issues that most musicians would be afraid to approach. "I don't really feel that opening your heart makes you more vulnerable," she has said. And she proves that in every song she writes.

Many of Jewel's songs were poems first, but, as she points out, their true origins are in her emotions. It doesn't matter to her which comes first, the lyrics or the music; what is important is that the word or the note fits the emotion. She equates writing to "being alone in a dark room, blindfolded. Your mind will still give you color and emotion, and you just need to find the word to match the emotion."

Jewel's instrumental arrangements are tasteful yet dramatic. A self-taught guitarist, she has developed an understated technique that makes an ideal palette for her vocal style. She utilizes textures and harmonics that call to mind the genius of Paul Simon and Joni Mitchell.

Jewel has a knack for fashioning guitar hooks that may seem innocuous at first but then get stuck in the listener's mind for days, providing an inspiring mental soundtrack. She plays with the texture of sound like the elderly couple in "Painters" plays with oils, enriching her life and ours with music that will last for generations to come.

Her chops—the purely technical skills involved in playing an instrument—aren't as sharp as they will eventually become, but she makes the most of what her hands allow, and her playing is getting stronger all the time. "Making music is a very visual process for me; it is almost like painting in my head. I just need to catch my hands up to that," she explains.

Of course the music and words wouldn't be quite so powerful were it not for her amazing voice, which sparkles with clarity and control. Critics tend to speak of innocence and wisdom as if the two qualities are mutually exclusive, but they are perfectly integrated in Jewel's voice (and in her life, for that matter).

She's able to evoke every conceivable emotion simply by varying the pitch and cadence of her singing. You can feel the sorrow and frustration in "Adrian," the giddy elation in "Morning Song," the disgust in "Pieces of You" and "Daddy," the heartbreak in "Foolish Games."

Like a stage actor—an area where Jewel has some experience—she doesn't just recite the words, she feels them in her bones and can communicate those feelings to the audience. This is perhaps the single quality she has most in common with Neil Young. There is very little difference between what Neil feels and what the listener hears, and the same is true of Jewel.

Of course, while Neil's voice is all about character, that's only one element of Jewel's soprano impact. A reviewer in *George* magazine noted, "Her voice is now a powerful and dramatic instrument, capable of holding notes past their breaking point." She utilizes sonic irony to evoke and provoke emotion, singing the most graphic sentiments in her sweetest voice, like in "God's Gift to Women" or "Daddy" or "Pieces of You."

She manipulates chromatic shapes by altering the stresses and accents in her vocal lines. Jewel's voice can be husky and throaty in midrange, crystal clear in the upper registers. She speeds up and slows down at will and to great effect.

A review in *US* magazine raved, "When she sings, her voice doesn't just follow the melody in a straight line but dips and soars all around it like an acrobat falling through the air, then somersaulting, then flying upward." Her vocal control is phenomenal, and her phrasing is vibrant and complex. Jewel will whisper, whoop, twang, and deliver a sexy alto in the course of a single song.

And don't forget the wild card in Jewel's deck of skills—she can yodel! "I used to begin shows with the yodel to get people's attention but I found it was a hard act to follow," she told *Now* magazine.

Back in early 1997, when Jewel was anticipating

the eventual release of her second CD, she told *Spin* magazine that there would be no yodeling on the disc because, as she put it, "It was taking all the attention away from my other songs." Jewel has said that she doesn't want to be known only as "the girl who yodels," and as everyone who has seen her cut loose on the Elton Britt tune "Chime Bells" can attest, it is an attention grabber.

Jewel introduces it to the crowd, saying something to the effect of "This is a song my daddy taught me when I used to weed the potato gardens as a little girl." The audience members who know what's coming cheer wildly in anticipation, and the others are in for a special surprise.

Accompanying herself on the guitar, strumming with furious energy, Jewel belts out a fun, souped-up rendition of the sweet old song. Charming lyrics and a lighthearted delivery—including a kiss blown to the audience—are interspersed with yodeling parts. The song is a quick one, lasting only a couple of minutes, and it seems even more brief due to the speed with which it's delivered. "Should I go faster?" Jewel teases the fans, who roar with approval. Faster and faster she sings, like a flat stone skipping across a glacial lake, yet every note is as clear as a chime bell.

It's a sight and sound that must be seen and heard to be fully appreciated. Perhaps when she gets a few more CDs under her belt and feels more established, Jewel will include "Chime Bells" on a studio release. Or perhaps it could be included on a live project.

Of course, her reluctance to overdo the yodeling is understandable. As an artist, Jewel doesn't want to be pigeonholed as a novelty act any more than she wants to be labeled as a folksinger. "If you'd seen an earlier show, you'd say I was rock," Jewel once asserted in *Spin*. "People think I'm some kind of hippie."

One of the first lessons a songwriter learns is that people often don't listen closely to the music, treating it like air freshener rather than art. That can lead to misunderstandings when one is singing about controversial subjects in a subtle way. For example, to this day there are folks who take the verses of Randy Newman's "Short People" at face value, not grasping the satire of bigotry that he intended to convey.

Many of Jewel's songs tend to be rather lyrically complex. One of the virtues of having stripped-down musical arrangements and an ultra-clear singing voice is that the words are intelligible if the listener is paying attention. Too bad that doesn't always happen.

One evening in a Detroit coffee shop, a group of people who were casually listening while Jewel was singing "Pieces of You," stormed out of the room when she got to the "faggot" part, having misunderstood that the song is an ironic indictment of bigotry, not an endorsement. The bigger irony is that critics have taken Jewel to task for being simplistic. "I guess it's not simplistic enough," Jewel has said in reply.

Another misconception among casual listeners is that Jewel is all sweetness and light, either musically or otherwise. Perhaps that false impression is based partly on her Nordic looks, the unabashed clarity of her vocal style, or her poetic references to hope and angels. Jewel isn't afraid to be innocent or feminine, traits that can be misinterpreted as signs of weakness.

She seems to be self-deprecatingly defensive at times, like when she sarcastically referred to the "problems of us rich white girls" on the Rosie O'Donnell show, as if she needs to apologize for the way certain narrow-minded critics might see her. A person usually makes that type of reflexive, preemptive first strike when trying to diffuse potential criticism. Jewel should never need to justify her life or her music as if she were "Michelle Shocked with a clothing allowance," as one writer put it.

Truth be told, the reality is a diametrical opposite of those perceptions. Jewel may not come across as cynical—that's what Courtney Love is for—but she recognizes pain and darkness in the world, and she often trains her observant heart on those subjects. An early review of *Pieces of You* in *Addicted to Noise* explained: "Jewel's lyrics can be as brutal as any in the Nineties. She just doesn't need to growl them."

In a review for the *Boston Herald*, "It's easy to be superficial about Jewel. With her blonde good looks and offhand, earthy/innocent sensuality, you expect her to sing 'Smelly Cat,' the favorite tune of *Friends* flake Phoebe." The review went on to explain that a deeper inspection revealed Jewel to be "an engaging, unpretentious performer."

Jewel's increasing forays into electric guitar and full ensemble arrangements figure to help her shake the annoying neo-folk label that seems to cling to her dress like the proverbial sticky valentine. Her in-concert version of the Patti Smith classic "Dancing Barefoot" is proof that Jewel can rock hard.

The premier female poet-rocker of the seventies, Smith appeared on bills with groups such as Television and the Ramones at the New York venue CBGBs. "Dancing Barefoot" is one of the most frequently covered songs among modern musicians. The tune has an upbeat feel that can be delivered bouncy or gritty. Jewel's version usually starts with moderate intensity and builds to a frenzied finish.

The lyrics are a hymnlike testament to the joys and dangers of love and freedom, subject matter that Jewel is fond of exploring. Jewel hammers out the vocals with the fierce intensity of a person who has lived the lyrics but kept them bottled up inside for too long. Anyone who has seen Jewel rock on "Dancing Barefoot" should grasp the fact

that she is much more than just a sweet litle girl
with an acoustic guitar.

Unfortunately, when Jewel isn't being falsely portrayed as a granola girl, she all too often gets treated
like a sex object. Which is not to say that she is
striving for an androgynous image; that's clearly not
the case. "I adore the human experience, I really
adore the darkness. I don't mind being sexy and girl-
ish and womanly and all those things at the same
time. I like our rough edges," she told Lauren Hutton during a televised interview.

It isn't exactly going out on a limb to say that
Jewel is a knockout. Her physical presence mirrors
her voice: womanly, yet with disarming innocence. Her green eyes, perfect skin, and full lips
are enchanting enough on their own, but mix
in her va-va-voom figure and you've got quite
a package. Suzan Colon described Jewel in *Details*, as "a little dish of pancakes [read: short and
stacked]."

Curvy and doll faced, Jewel has the look that
MTV was created to market, and there is no question that nature's endowments have had a positive
effect on her career. But like the fame it helps create, the beauty thing is a mixed bag. The same
physical gifts that attract superficial attention can
distract from deeper accomplishments. In that regard it was both frustrating and amusing for Jewel
to experience the way the media drooled over her

1997 Grammy Awards photos like hungry hyenas at a fresh kill.

As you've no doubt seen or heard already, the dress Jewel wore for the show turned out to be virtually translucent. When she went onstage to present an award with actor Kevin Spacey, the spotlights revealed aspects of Jewel that weren't meant for the viewing audience.

Suddenly the highlights of the event, her breasts were given full coverage in the press. The pictures have circulated on the Internet, and they cropped up again in the year-end issue of *Playboy* magazine, among others.

Jewel later explained, to little effect, that she had donned the dress in a poorly lit room and didn't notice the see-through quality. She seemed taken aback by all the fuss, telling a *Detroit Free Press* reporter, "If you're a spiritual person, people are scared if you look sexy one night."

A *NY Rock* writer Otto Luck chimed in with this sound advice for Jewel: "Should anybody discredit you for possessing god's gift of beauty . . . why not respond with these simple words: 'Eat your heart out, baby.' "

A writer in L.A.'s *New Times* magazine cheered Jewel on, saying, "She's no longer a dressed-down folk singer; now she's a pop star dressed in a take-a-good-look-at-these-nipples gown."

Jewel is more than familiar with the light and dark sides of being beautiful. She related this story to journalist Julene Snyder from the days when she was struggling in San Diego: "I was desperate for a job and I saw this kid playing in a strip mall coffee shop called Java Joe's. So I asked if I could have a job and the boss said yeah. Then he asked if I'd pose naked for his calendar. Oh God, here we go again!"

Jewel being Jewel, she managed to get the gig without getting undressed. And, out of sheer necessity, she's grown ever more adept at coping with the ardently amorous males who are drawn like moths to her shows.

There was the time a would-be suitor called out "I love you, Jewel" during the first notes of "Don't," causing her to botch a chord. Never one to ignore her fans, she replied, "I know, but I hate it when you do that. I always get so embarrassed. Thank you, though."

Trouble is, those raging hormones don't always make their presence known quite so innocuously, i.e., the spaz who yelled "Take it off!" at the Beacon Theater in New York City, prompting Jewel to improvise an extra part in "Pieces of You" about "stupid boys."

There was a hilarious moment at the Orpheum when Jewel made a spicy gesture in reply to an inappropriate offer from an audience member. The largely female crowd erupted with laughter and approval.

Jewel addresses testosterone-fueled piggishness in such songs as "Race Car Driver" and "God's Gift to Women." She injects humor into the subject while getting her point across.

God's Gift to Women

Also known as "My Own Private God's Gift to Women," which is the primary line in the chorus, this song is as funny as it is cathartic. It candidly (and explicitly) sums up all the rancor women have built up from being manhandled by overly aggressive Romeos. Along with the sarcastic title, Jewel manages to work in a sly reference to Carly Simon's "You're So Vain."

Race Car Driver

"Race Car Driver" would make a nice flip-side to "God's Gift to Women," as it gently takes apart another kind of creepy male. This type initially thinks he's going to seduce Jewel with his hot rod, so to speak, but when that doesn't work he turns into a sensitive, '90s kind of guy. No (fuzzy) dice. Says our heroine, he's still "a real small man in a real big car."

So, as with everything else, there are positive and negative aspects to being beautiful, and Jewel is simply trying to keep her head on straight. "I try not to play on my sexuality," she asserted in *Q* magazine. "I love words and turns of phrase—to me, that's sexy. It's easy to believe others are beautiful and much harder to believe you are. But at the same time, you are aware of yourself."

It would be impossible not to be aware of yourself when you are voted Sexiest Female Artist (ahead of Fiona Apple and Courtney Love) in a *Rolling Stone* readers' poll, as Jewel recently was.

Without question, it is disturbing that the predictions of musicians from over a decade ago (Huey Lewis, no less!)—that worthy artists would be ignored because they have acne—are now accepted realities. But the bottom line is that there have always been sex symbols in popular music; the popularity part has never been purely about music.

Artists such as Jewel, Jakob Dylan (of the Wallflowers), country songstress Shania Twain, and Gavin Rossdale (of Bush) were all musicians before they became sex symbols. If they weren't legitimate artists, people would be buying their magazine covers—not their CDs.

However one feels about fashion's place in rock 'n' roll, it would be twice as pretentious for Jewel to play down her sex appeal as it is for her to wear lip gloss and Prada. As in every other phase of her life, she is simply making her own choices and trying to make the most of every second she has in this world. Sometimes she's one thing, sometimes she's another, and anyone who tries to limit her is going to be left shouting into empty space.

Joan Anderman summed it up nicely in the *Phoenix*, describing Jewel as a "gen Xer who doesn't trade in anger and angst, and a polished, proficient vocalist who hits bad notes 'cause they feel right. She's a sweet girl who flips off obnoxious fans. She wrote a punk song and sang a lullaby. Jewel yodels, sexily. Now that's cool."

> ### "I believe we are divine by nature."
> —Jewel in *Big Shout*

Perhaps the strongest aspect of Jewel's character is her spirituality. These days it takes courage to admit that you have faith in anything that isn't corporal. (Oddly enough, that word comes from the doctrine that the bread of the Eucharist represents the body of Christ, but it has come to also describe anything that is strictly of the nonspiritual, material world.)

Personal faith is a subject that is so intrinsically, well . . . *personal*, that any attempt to delve into another person's beliefs is fraught with potential pitfalls. Nevertheless, it is safe to say that Jewel is very spiritual, a fact that shines through in her words and music. She has mentioned that she prays and has said that she was raised as a Mormon until age eight, the year in which her parents divorced.

* * *

Her first exposure to organized religion came at an early age. The following excerpt from a June '96 *Spin* magazine article, in which Jewel cajoles her way into the garden of a Mormon temple, reveals an interesting bit of information: " 'My dad was a Mormon,' she tells (the people at the temple), conveniently omitting the part about his excommunication."

Jewel's song "Nikos," the story of a boy child born out of wedlock, written in first person from his half-sister's point of view, contains the line: "My daddy got excommunicated from the Mormon church." "Nikos" is one of Jewel's most poignant and straightforward compositions.

Mormonism, a sect of Christianity founded in the 1800s, is based primarily on the doctrines of the Bible and *The Book of Mormon*. Among the Mormon ethics is the belief that God is a material being and that humans can become divine. Mormons are known for their independence and work ethic.

Although she does not belong to any branch of institutionalized religion, Jewel has often made pronouncements of spiritual faith rooted firmly in humanistic soil. In her words, "We are each other's angels in the way that we answer each other's prayers and we can also make each other's lives miserable."

Growing up in Alaska obviously played a part in

the shaping of Jewel's intuitive system of belief. "I'm not religious, but I am a very faithful person. I'm very spiritual and when you are raised among that much beauty . . . you can't help but believe in humanity," she affirms.

Surviving some of the hard times in her childhood and the lean months of living hand-to-mouth as a nineteen-year-old in San Diego also had an impact on how she views the divine aspects of life. "I believe that in my loneliest moments I have not been alone," she has stated. Jewel mentions angels in "Amen," "I'm Sensitive," "Emily," and "Angel Standing By." She also makes joking reference to the "angel bumper" on her car, which protects her from her own erratic driving.

Probably the seminal expression of Jewel's concern for the human spirit is "Who Will Save Your Soul," her first single. It speaks to the way modern people have become cast adrift from their own capacity for spirituality. "No wonder people are stuffing themselves with TV and drugs and sex. They're trying to fill that void," Jewel elaborates. The companion video to "Who Will Save Your Soul" takes place in a bathroom, which might seem incongruous until you hear Jewel explain the reasoning behind it: "When I was a little girl in Alaska, I used to go outdoors a lot. That's how I got to know God, find beauty and simplicity. I got to be with myself and have silence around me. So now, because my days are so full with people and meetings, constantly, I go into the bathroom to be alone."

That, in many respects, is a perfect distillation of everything there is to love about Jewel. She's so grounded in the everyday—"earthy," as the pundits say. She taps into the soulfulness of a place— the water closet—that few theologians would care to consider "the last sacred place on Earth," as Jewel calls it. In that respect she is the definitive Everyday Angel.

CHAPTER FIFTEEN

❦

Other Voices

Although there was an old piano at the Homer homestead and plenty of music and singing in Jewel's childhood, she doesn't recall the Kilcher household as being the type where the stereo was always on. In fact, she once told *US* magazine, "I've never been a real music fan. I'm odd that way."

Actually it isn't that unusual for a gifted songwriter not to be an audiophile, especially early on. Over the past several years Jewel has undergone an awakening in terms of her awareness of modern music. When she first arrived in San Diego, she was literally hard pressed to distinguish the Beatles from the Rolling Stones, but that no longer applies.

Her current tastes, which are constantly expanding and being refined, range from Yma Sumac to Leo Kottke to k.d. lang to Jennifer Warnes. Many of her musical influences are fairly recent discoveries, with the notable exception of the jazz and blues artists she's loved since high school: Ella Fitzgerald, Etta James, Muddy Waters, Howlin' Wolf, Nina Simone, among others.

Jewel has dipped into the Cole Porter songbook, and she cites him as a songwriting role model. Jewel has also been known to do a dramatic reading of the Gershwin standard "Summertime" to open her concerts.

She is an avid Aretha Franklin admirer. "One day, when I grow up, maybe I'll be half as good as Aretha," Jewel opined when the "Queen of Soul" sang "The Star-Spangled Banner" at the Democratic National Convention.

In the classical vein, Jewel admits to singing from the operas of Giacomo Puccini *(La Boheme, Madama Butterfly)* in the shower. She has also mentioned Claudio Monteverdi, who is considered the first great composer in the history of opera. Jewel's time at Interlochen went a long way toward cultivating her feel for opera and baroque classical.

Jewel's favorite baroque composer is, not surprisingly, Antonio Vivaldi *(The Four Seasons)*, but she also enjoys the work of Sir Edward Elgar, who composed *Enigma Variations*. Among recent classical works, Aaron Copeland's *All the Blue Horses* has seen action in Jewel's CD player.

Jewel credits Steve Poltz for helping turn her ear toward some of the big bands of the 1930s and

'40s—the music of Benny Goodman, Glenn Miller, et al.—not to mention contemporary artists in various genres.

One of the qualities that made the late Kurt Cobain a musician's musician was his compulsion to promote the work of bands he loved (the Raincoats, the Meat Puppets), and Jewel seems to have a similar drive. She has mentioned the following musicians, among others:

The Replacements

The archetypal midwestern punk band, the Minneapolis-based Replacements churned out edgy, drunken, heartfelt rock 'n' roll with an undercurrent of down-home feel. In many ways—particularly with regard to humorous and drunken behavior—they were the forefathers of the Rugburns. Insightful, empathetic lyrics and barbed musical hooks are songsmith Paul Westerberg's forte. Jewel has mentioned *Let It Be* and *Pleased to Meet Me* (which she notes is "great on both Saturday nights and Sunday mornings") as personal favorites.

Tracy Chapman

Also "discovered" in a coffeehouse (in Boston), Chapman, who tends to take long leaves of absence from the music scene, scored a hit with "Fast Car" before Jewel had even picked up a guitar. The understandably starstruck Jewel has said, "When she walks by, I'm like: 'aaaaaaaah, it's Tracy Chapman!'" Jewel used to cover Chapman's "Behind the Wall" in the early days at the Innerchange.

Joni Mitchell

In the first year or so following the release of *Pieces of You*, Jewel was lumped with just about every female singer-songwriter who'd ever lived, but none more frequently than Joni Mitchell, specifically her album *Blue*. Ironically, Jewel claims not to have even heard Joni Mitchell prior to making *Pieces of You*. Her bluesy but sweet soprano and soulful poetry of strength and self-doubt made her the definitive female voice in late-sixties folk pop.

Rickie Lee Jones

In the July 1997 issue of *Mojo* magazine, Jewel tagged *Rickie Lee Jones* as being her favorite CD at the time. Jones, like Jewel, was once touted as the natural successor to Joni Mitchell. Something else they have in common is their ability to shift from world weary to innocent in the course of a single vocal line.

Nanci Griffith

A folk-country-pop songwriter with Texas roots and a voice like a songbird's, Griffith has a loyal following (particularly in the U.K.), winning a Grammy in 1994 for *Other Voices, Other Rooms*, a collection of covers. Jewel has said she is "always amazed" by Griffith's ability to sing about the darkest subjects in the sweetest of voices, a technique that Jewel, too, employs with powerful results.

Asked by *Rolling Stone* to pick her five favorite releases of 1997, Jewel put together a list that reflects Steve Poltz's influence and the growth of Jewel's musical knowledge:

1. *OK Computer* by Radiohead
2. *Brighten the Corners* by Pavement
3. *El Corazon* by Steve Earle
4. *Time Out of Mind* by Bob Dylan
5. *Surfacing* by Sarah MacLachlan

Interestingly, Jewel's life has been filled with books as much, if not more than, music. Her love of the printed word runs deep, and she reads a range of authors from Annie Dillard to Dr. Seuss. Among her favorite writers she has cited are:

Pablo Neruda

An acclaimed poet from the South American country of Chile, Neruda won the Nobel Prize for literature in 1971. His early poetry, which has been of particular interest to Jewel, is very personal and focused on love and despair.

Kurt Vonnegut, Jr.

In novels such as *Slaughterhouse Five* and *Cat's Cradle*, Vonnegut mixes science fiction and social criticism with humor and empathy to paint landscapes of the twentieth century. Jewel has mentioned *Welcome to the Monkeyhouse* as her favorite of his works.

Henry Miller and Anaïs Nin

One of the world's most famous literary couples, Miller *(Tropic of Cancer)* and Nin *(A Spy in the House of Love)* had a ten-year affair in Paris and America. Jewel mentions them in "Morning Song," and she has echoed the romantic "Morning Song" referral in interviews, noting that her early days in San Diego felt similar to what she imagined Paris was like in the days of Henry and Anaïs.

Plato

Greek philosopher Plato was a student of Socrates and a teacher of Aristotle. Jewel has long been compelled by the idea of immortality, a subject that is addressed in Plato's dialogues. Of particular interest to Jewel are the theories of beauty and art found in the *Symposium*. She was captivated by the concepts of pure reason, but she soon came to realize that these theories hadn't taken into account the glories and foibles of the human body and thus were incomplete. While at Interlochen, Jewel was allowed to teach a philosophy class, and she focused much study on the work of Plato.

Charles Bukowski

A prolific poet who lived hard and wrote even harder, Bukowski was immortalized in the film *Barfly* and the poem *An Evening with Charles Bukowski* by Raymond Carver. He is perhaps Jewel's strongest poetic influence, and she has written a poem about meeting his widow.

Bukowski once wrote: "You begin saving the world by saving one man at a time; all else is grandiose romanticism or politics." That is a statement that nicely sums up much of what Jewel loves about his work; he maintains a poetic sensibility and a pragmatic optimism in dark times. Jewel said in *New Musical Express*, "I never thought I was a poet. Bukowski's a poet! Jesus, I'm a kid living in a car!"

Marcel Proust

One of the great French writers of the 1920s, he is best known for the multivolume novel *Remembrance of Things Past*. In his worldview, art is essentially a religious pursuit, the noblest of humankind's endeavors. This is a concept that very much appeals to Jewel.

Fyodor Dostoyevsky

The ideas of the brilliant Russian novelist who wrote *The Brothers Karamozov*, (among others), regarding the inability of modern science to fulfill people's spiritual needs, are reflected in many of Jewel's poems and songs.

CHAPTER SIXTEEN

❧

Rockin' in the Free World

One of the pinnacle points in Jewel's amazing three-year rise to fame were the weeks she spent on tour with Lilith Fair. The most talked about concert tour of summer 1997, Lilith Fair was an all-female traveling rock 'n' roll show that was the brainchild of Sarah MacLachlan.

Lilith, who was Adam's first wife according to Hebrew legend, told her husband, "I will not be submissive to you." Fair has three meanings that fit the spirit of the event: beautiful; free of prejudice; and an exhibit that acquaints the public with a product. Organized by the brilliant twenty-nine-year-old singer-songwriter MacLachlan, the concept came about when she and Paula Cole were on tour together in 1995.

Incredibly, the two artists found there was resistance among promoters to the idea of having two women on the same bill. But when the two artists saw how enthusiastically the crowds reacted, they realized the potential for a full-scale all-female tour. MacLachlan pursued the idea and brought it to life.

Lilith featured a rotating lineup of more than sixty female artists. They included: Fiona Apple, Mary Black, Tracy Chapman, Paula Cole, Sheryl Crow, Joan Osborne, Suzanne Vega, and Cassandra Wilson, a virtual who's who of the top women in rock.

Jewel joined the tour for two stints: a week in early July and the first three weeks of August. Both the fans and the media acclaimed her performances as highlights of the festival. One of the thrilling aspects of her appearances was her adventures in amplification: Jewel often went electric at Lilith, playing an ebony colored Gibson electric guitar.

Her performance in Toronto, as the tour was drawing near its end, was typically superb. Jewel joined the Indigo Girls onstage for their song "Galileo," and her yodeling added an entirely new dimension. When her turn came to take over the stage, Jewel and her fully electric ensemble uplifted the rain-soaked crowd with a great set that featured high-energy versions of "You Were Meant for Me" and "Who Will Save Your Soul," plus a heartwrenchingly intense "Foolish Games."

After a terrific set by Sarah MacLachlan, Jewel and the rest of the Lilith performers got together to sing Joni Mitchell's "Big Yellow Taxi." A folk-rock classic, it speaks to the way people often don't appreciate what's good in life until they lose it. Hopefully, the Lilith Fair will be with us for many summers to come.

Jewel said of her Lilith Fair experience, "Usually you're so lonely on the road, like a little astronaut. We had a real sense of community. None of us wanted to leave."

For an American artist steeped in American music tradition, making a splash in Europe may be a secondary concern. But for Jewel, the goal is always to reach as many listeners as she can, no matter what country they call home.

To date, overseas sales of *Pieces of You* have been phenomenal:

Canada	5,000,000+
New Zealand	4,000,000+
Australia	3,000,000+
Singapore	1,000,000+

The CD has been certified Gold in Japan, Malaysia, Taiwan, Indonesia, the Philippines, Norway, and Spain.

Although she'd been on the road for much of the three years since the release of her debut CD, Jewel had never toured Asia. That changed in late September 1997, when she flew into the Taipei, Taiwan, airport.

She was met there by dozens of paparazzi, the

freelance photographers who pursue celebrities in hopes of getting candid pictures that they can sell to publishers. The next morning, Jewel's face graced the cover of practically every newspaper in the country. Like any tourist in an exotic land, she visited the local museums and landmarks. She even had her palm read by a sweet elderly man on the street.

From there it was off to Japan, where Jewel performed in concert and on TV and radio for the people of Osaka and Tokyo. Situated on an inlet of the Pacific Ocean, Osaka is a port city with a population of about two and a half million. Tokyo, the capital city of Japan, is also located on an inlet of the Pacific. It is home to almost twelve million citizens. It was a mutual love affair between Jewel and the audiences of the Far East.

When she wasn't sightseeing, playing, or sleeping, Jewel took advantage of the chance to sample the incredible sushi of the Pacific Rim. A traditional Japanese food that has swelled in popularity in America over the past two decades, sushi is a general term for a variety of dishes that feature raw fish as the main element. Jewel loves sushi, and she asserts that the sushi she's had in her home state of California is as good as what she had in the birthplace of sushi, Japan.

Jewel departed Japan after two weeks and traveled to Europe; it was her third trip to the continent. She wowed fans in England, Scotland, France, Sweden, Germany, and Italy.

Jewel's next stop, in early November, was Spain. It was her first visit to that country, and she celebrated with a concert at the Tivoli Theater in honor of the grand opening of the Hard Rock Cafe in Barcelona. The following day she was at the Hard Rock in Madrid. From Spain, Jewel traveled on to the Netherlands and Belgium. The crowds belonged to her, and she blew them away in city after city.

On January 25, 1998, Jewel sang the national anthem prior to Super Bowl XXXII in San Diego. In a statement made before the game, Jewel said, "San Diego has been my home for the past five years, and it's exciting that the Super Bowl is coming back here for the first time in a decade."

What turned out to be really exciting was the sight of Jewel putting her hand over her heart, perhaps in part to compensate for the dramatic décolletage of her blouse. The anthem was prerecorded and lip-synched by Jewel, which is standard procedure for the Super Bowl, but it seemed to start before she was ready—she was in the process of waving to the crowd.

Still, her incredible voice made a very difficult song sound effortless. Those tabbed in the past to do the pre–Super Bowl anthem include Whitney

Houston, Billy Joel, Garth Brooks, and Diana Ross.
Jewel's performance was viewed by an estimated
100 million TV viewers worldwide.

CHAPTER SEVENTEEN

What's Next

There is practically no limit to Jewel's creative energy, and it sometimes seems as if she was born to perform. So nobody who knows her was surprised when she dove headfirst into acting, despite having had minimal experience or training.

Jewel is slated to make her feature film debut as the female lead in *To Live On*, a Civil War drama that press releases describe as "*Platoon* in America."

The screenplay, written by James Schamus, is based on the novel *Woe to Live On* by Daniel Woodrell, which was published in 1987. The film will be directed by Ang Lee, who received acclaim for his direction of *Sense and Sensibility*. He also directed *Eat Drink Man Woman*, *The Wedding Banquet*, and *The Ice Storm*.

Jewel will play the love interest of two young soldiers—played by Skeet Ulrich *(Scream)* and Toby Maguire *(The Ice Storm)*—whose lives are changed forever while engaged in battle on the Kansas-Missouri border. Much of the action centers on the 1863 burning of Lawrence, Kansas, and its aftermath.

The film is scheduled to begin shooting in March 1998 in Missouri. The subject came up during her February appearance on Rosie O'Donnell's show, and Jewel seemed to approach the project with understandable excitement *and* trepidation.

She facetiously said that there was "no pressure." Considering that the more Jewel worries, the better things tend to come out for her, people will probably be talking about an Oscar nomination a year or so from now.

Although she has never appeared on the big screen, Jewel isn't a total stranger to acting. She appeared in a benefit production of the *Wizard of Oz*, playing the lead role of Dorothy. Jewel's involvement came about when the producers, Darrell Larson and John Brauer, heard her on National Public Radio's *All Things Considered* one afternoon in July 1995.

The performance took place on November 5, 1995, at New York City's Lincoln Center, and it aired on TNT television the night before Thanksgiving. Jewel went the full route, doing plenty of dancing, singing, and speaking. Other performers included Jackson Browne as the Scarecrow and Roger Daltry as the Tin Man. Jewel played a guitar duet of "Over the Rainbow" with enigmatic genius

Ry Cooder. "It's gorgeous, I can't believe I get to play with him," Jewel gleefully reported.

A video and CD of the one-time event is available, with proceeds going to the Children's Defense Fund, which lobbies for the needs of American children, particularly the disabled and the poor.

Jewel found the stage experience "very satisfying," but also speculated that she would prefer the big screen. "Less redundancy," as she put it.

Jewel has already recorded her second CD, and it is scheduled for release sometime in mid-1998. The release date has changed numerous times since the initial recording sessions took place. Atlantic has kept the project under tight cover, creating a lot of speculation about Jewel's new CD.

Rumor has it that the title will be *Fritz Creek Store*, which was a log-cabin general store near the Kilcher family's homestead. A black-and-white photograph reportedly exists of Jewel, age four, and one of her brothers in front of the store, and there's a good chance that this will constitute the cover art.

The success of "Foolish Games," which caused a resurgence in sales of *Pieces of You*, was largely responsible for the delay. But it isn't as if the new work was completely in the can and ready to ship out. In fact, Jewel was back in the studio in late 1997 to do more recording.

Word was, some of the finished tracks had "missed the mark." Jewel also felt that the lag between recording the CD and releasing it would create an incomplete picture of where she is artistically.

"I think it's going to show a lot of growth," Jewel told a *Boston Globe* writer back in 1996, talking about the new CD. Incredibly, over four years have melted away since Jewel first came on the scene. If you're old enough to do so, think of how much you changed (and grew, hopefully) from age nineteen to age twenty-four.

Because she has material for at least a dozen CDs—and has had for quite a while—we aren't likely to get a release of entirely new songs anytime soon. But that doesn't matter much since her treatment of the older work will undoubtedly reflect where she is at the moment.

When she first started getting national exposure, Jewel blanched at the "folksy" label that was strapped onto her like a saddle by the music press. *Pieces of You* is inescapably steeped in the American folk tradition, but Jewel is much more than a coffeehouse warbler. Her upcoming release is certain to show a new level of sonic complexity.

"I think you have to layer your work," she explained in a *Seattle Times* article, "put in stuff for people to find down the line. If you don't, well, that shoots longevity in the foot."

Jewel's voice is more mature than it was when

Pieces of You was recorded. Her hands have gotten stronger, so she's gotten better at narrowing the gap between what she wants to express with a guitar and what she can express. She also has studio experience under her belt, which should make this a more self-assured effort. "I look at my first album as a pencil sketch and this one is more of a skilled drawing," she said in *Spin*.

The supporting musicians—some of the most respected studio heavyweights in music—are T-Bone Wolk (*Saturday Night Live,* Hall & Oates) on bass, Jerry Marotta (Peter Gabriel, Indigo Girls) on drums, Marc Shulman (Elvis Costello) on guitar, and Michael Blair (Lou Reed) playing percussion.

The producer is Peter Collins, who has worked with an eclectic mix of artists and styles, from Rush and Genesis to the Indigo Girls and Nanci Griffith. "Peter's real talent is making everybody sound like themselves," said Jewel.

The recording studio at Bearsville is aesthetically rustic and quaint and chock-full of history. Acts that have cut records or mixed them there include R.E.M., Metallica, Phish, Suzanne Vega, and The Band. The mixing board that the Who used for *Quadrophenia* is also on the premises. During the process of rehearsing and recording, Jewel lived in the house that Robbie Robertson, guitarist for The Band, once owned.

Jewel's mom was at Bearsville during the time of

recording, as was Jewel's boyfriend, Michel Francoeur. (He's tall, dark, tattooed, and handsome; hails from Quebec, Canada; speaks with a French accent; and works as a male model.) Nedra Carroll believes that it is important for a young artist such as her daughter to have a strong network of support, not only within the record company but also among friends, family, and the like.

Among the songs that were recorded for *Fritz Creek Store* are:

"Absence of Fear"
"Boy Needs a Bike"
"Buttercup"
"Carnivore"
"Deep Water"
"Face of Love"
"Fading Away"
"Fragile Flame"
"Fritz Creek Store"
"Gray Matter"
"Innocence Maintained"
"Jessica"
"Louisa and Her Blue Guitar"
"Love Me Just Leave Me Alone"
"Moon over Austin"
"Nicotine Love"
"Nikos"
"Run Tonto Run"

"Satellite"
"Sometimes It Be That Way"
"1,000 Miles Away"
"Tough Girl"

Any of these songs could make or fail to make the final cut. Expect at least half the songs to have full-band arrangements; there were multiple versions done of at least three of the tunes. As for which will be released as singles, we'll just have to wait and see.

One certainty is that Red Hot Chili Peppers bassist Flea will be making at least one contribution and probably more. Jewel notes that he "does an awesome bass line" on "Satellite," and she calls it "my favorite song on the record." She wrote it during preproduction.

"Satellite" is not a cover of the Dave Matthews tune of the same name. Jewel says, "It's about that a lot of us are taught to program our VCRs but not to understand our emotions. We know how to send satellites into space but we don't know how to relate to each other."

Flea also worked his magic on "Face of Love," "Innocence Maintained," and a few others. Flea and Jewel first met while Jewel was still living in her van. Flea was suffering from a cold at the time, and he calls seeing Jewel an "oasis." He introduced himself, they started talking, and Jewel asked if she could play him some of her songs. Flea recalls, "Ya know, when someone says they're going to play you some songs, the first thing I think about is running in terror. But, she did it and it was just so incredibly beautiful."

He gave Jewel encouragement, and they stayed in touch over the years. When he heard she was working on her second release, he offered to chip in.

Considering her extraordinarily rapid rise to fame, along with the fact that her adventurous life makes for a great story, it was only a matter of time before Jewel signed a book deal.

No fewer than eight of the major New York publishing houses engaged in a bidding war to acquire the right to publish a scrapbook memoir of her life, with HarperCollins coming out on top. She has also put together a volume of her poetry. Jewel has often asserted that her poetry is more personal and autobiographical than her songs, so the release of this collection is anxiously anticipated by her fans. Jewel will make a reported two million dollars to chronicle her twenty-four years in poetry, prose, and pictures.

This is a landmark scenario in at least a couple of ways. First, of the six billion people on the planet Earth, not many have been paid to write a book about the first third or so of their existence. Second, even the biggest names in show business aren't necessarily advanced an amount equal to what Jewel commanded after such a short time on the national scene. Also, the inclusion of poetry in a book deal of any financial significance is extremely rare.

Once again, Jewel's success has been a direct result of her courage in living from the heart and following her dream. She's faced the world head on, done more in less time than most folks ever will, and is reaping the rewards.

CHAPTER EIGHTEEN

Bringing It All Back Home

"I've always felt very alone and very
suffocated, and to actually be so blessed
as to live a dream, I find to be an honor."
—Jewel

"I believed that I was worth something,
that I shouldn't have to compromise
my pride and my health to have
a roof over my head."
—Jewel

Everyone's life is a work in progress. So how
do you end a book about a person whose story
has really just begun? Jewel has obviously lived
and learned more than most in her first twenty-
four years, but she'll no doubt continue to grow
and change, and her work is bound to reflect that
development.

The constant—the thing that Jewel fans can always trust will be a part of her music—is Jewel's innate desire to celebrate humanity and connect with everyone through her art. As she said in *Melody Maker*, "I love people. I love every f*#ked up and beautiful thing about us." The important issue for us, as fans, to consider is what we can do to reflect and magnify that empathy for our fellow creatures, either through work or art or just everyday acts of kindness. Jewel and Nedra are leading by example by starting a charity called Common Ground that will be devoted to worthy causes.

Jewel hopes that her fans take similar actions from the heart, both on behalf of others and for themselves. As she said in *Time*, "People look at me in magazines and feel like I'm a phenomenon, as if what I've accomplished is beyond their ability. I tell them to knock it off. If you respect what I've done, then do something yourself."

APPENDIX

Career Chronology

The following is a short time line of significant moments in Jewel's career to date.

October 1993–July 1994
Weekly gigs at the Innerchange, San Diego

March 1994
Signs contract with Atlantic Records

April 1994
Atlantic showcase at Film Center Cafe, New York City

July 28–29, 1994
Pieces of You live recording sessions at the Innerchange

August 21–26, 1994
Pieces of You studio recording sessions at Redwood
Digital Facility, Woodside, California

January 1995
West Coast residency

January 21, 1995
Final show at the Innerchange

February 1995
East Coast residency

February 28, 1995
Pieces of You released

March 2, 1995
Pieces of You release party at the Hahn Cosmopolitan Theater, San Diego

March 1995
Midwest and Toronto residency

May 10, 1995
Opens for Bob Dylan (afternoon), San Diego; Peter Murphy (evening), Los Angeles

May 15, 1995
Makes first appearance on Conan O'Brien show

October 1995
Opens for Deep Blue Something; Catherine Wheel and Belly

November 5, 1995
The Wizard of Oz taping at Lincoln Center, New York City

December 1995
Opens for John Hiatt

December 26, 1995
Makes first appearance on *The Tonight Show*

April 13, 1996
First of five dates opening for Bob Dylan

April 22, 1996
Makes first appearance on *Late Night with David Letterman*

May 1996
Pieces of You certified Gold (500,000 copies sold)

May 3, 1996
Opening date of first headlining tour, San Francisco

July 1996
Rehearsing and recording next CD

July 18–19, 1996
Jewelstock (free concert for fan club)

August 1996
Pieces of You certified Platinum (1,000,000 copies sold)

September 4, 1996
MTV Video Music Awards

September 1996
On tour in Australia

October 1996
On tour in Europe

January 20, 1997
Inaugural Ball, Washington, D.C.

January 28, 1997
American Music Awards

February 26, 1997
Grammy Awards

May 7, 1997
MTV *Unplugged* taping (aired 6/24)

May 10, 1997
Appears on *Saturday Night Live*

May 1997
On tour in Europe

August 1997
Lilith Fair

September 4, 1997
MTV Video Music Awards

October 1997
On tour in Japan and Europe

January 25, 1998
Performs national anthem at Super Bowl XXXI

February 1998
Grammy Awards

March 1998
Begins filming *To Live On*

May 1998
Publication of Jewel's book of poetry

GOLDEN BOY
The Matt Damon Story

by Kristen Busch

Golden Globe and Academy Award winner Matt Damon's meteoric rise to superstardom is the stuff of Hollywood legend. Only one year ago, hardly anyone had heard of Damon, despite an impressive list of film credits that included pivotal roles in *School Ties*, *Courage Under Fire*, and *The Rainmaker*. But with the release of *Good Will Hunting*, which he cowrote and costarred in with best friend Ben Affleck, Matt is everywhere.

And GOLDEN BOY tells the whole story: from his modest beginnings through his college years at Harvard and beyond to writing, selling, and starring in his own screenplay. It seems the sky is the limit for Damon—who has been linked with some of Hollywood's most beautiful young actresses! This is an insightful look at the life of this brilliant young writer, actor, and Academy Award winner.

Published by Ballantine Books.
Available wherever books are sold.

Hip Hop's "Daddy"

A FAMILY AFFAIR
The Unauthorized Sean "Puffy" Combs Story

by

Andrew Cable

Just how did one young kid from East Harlem revolutionize an entire industry? This candid and moving book tells all. From Sean Combs's birth in the projects to his life as a devoted father, from the phenomenal success of his multiplatinum album *No Way Out* to the founding of his Daddy House charity and his latest business ventures, A FAMILY AFFAIR reveals how this sexy, enterprising talent minted the hot genre known as hip hop soul and created a multimillion-dollar empire.

Published by Ballantine Books.
Available July 1998 in bookstores everywhere.

Don't miss a single one of these outstanding biographies.

Published by Ballantine Books. Available in your local bookstore.